I0427891

[H.A.S.C. No. 113–87]

INFORMATION TECHNOLOGY AND CYBER OPERATIONS: MODERNIZATION AND POLICY ISSUES IN A CHANGING NATIONAL SECURITY ENVIRONMENT

HEARING

BEFORE THE

SUBCOMMITTEE ON INTELLIGENCE, EMERGING THREATS AND CAPABILITIES

OF THE

COMMITTEE ON ARMED SERVICES HOUSE OF REPRESENTATIVES

ONE HUNDRED THIRTEENTH CONGRESS

SECOND SESSION

HEARING HELD
MARCH 12, 2014

U.S. GOVERNMENT PRINTING OFFICE

87–619   WASHINGTON : 2014

For sale by the Superintendent of Documents, U.S. Government Printing Office,
http://bookstore.gpo.gov. For more information, contact the GPO Customer Contact Center,
U.S. Government Printing Office. Phone 202–512–1800, or 866–512–1800 (toll-free). E-mail, gpo@custhelp.com.

CONTENTS

CHRONOLOGICAL LIST OF HEARINGS

2014

WEDNESDAY, MARCH 12, 2014

INFORMATION TECHNOLOGY AND CYBER OPERATIONS: MODERNIZATION AND POLICY ISSUES IN A CHANGING NATIONAL SECURITY ENVIRONMENT

STATEMENTS PRESENTED BY MEMBERS OF CONGRESS

WITNESSES

APPENDIX

INFORMATION TECHNOLOGY AND CYBER OPERATIONS: MODERNIZATION AND POLICY ISSUES IN A CHANGING NATIONAL SECURITY ENVIRONMENT

———————

HOUSE OF REPRESENTATIVES,
COMMITTEE ON ARMED SERVICES,
SUBCOMMITTEE ON INTELLIGENCE, EMERGING
THREATS AND CAPABILITIES,
Washington, DC, Wednesday, March 12, 2014.

The subcommittee met, pursuant to call, at 3:30 p.m., in room 2118, Rayburn House Office Building, Hon. Mac Thornberry (chairman of the subcommittee) presiding.

OPENING STATEMENT OF HON. MAC THORNBERRY, A REPRESENTATIVE FROM TEXAS, CHAIRMAN, SUBCOMMITTEE ON INTELLIGENCE, EMERGING THREATS AND CAPABILITIES

Mr. THORNBERRY. The subcommittee will come to order.

The subcommittee meets today to examine issues related to information technology [IT] and cyber operations, both from a policy and budget perspective.

We are glad to have both General Alexander and Ms. Takai back with us again this year.

These two issues are among the most challenging we face in national security.

On the first, the full committee and all subcommittees have undertaken a 2-year effort to improve the acquisition practices of the Department of Defense [DOD]. While there are improvements to be made in all areas of contracting and acquisition, there is particular concern about how the Department can put up-to-date technology in the hands of the warfighter in a timely and cost-effective manner.

This subcommittee has tried to keep a close watch on these issues over the years, but this broader reform effort, which we are pursuing cooperatively with the Senate and the Pentagon and industry, may give us opportunities to make improvements that have not been seriously pursued before, and we should take advantage of it.

The second issue, of course, is cyber operations. This subcommittee has viewed as one of its primary responsibilities helping ensure that the military is as prepared as it can be to defend the Nation in cyberspace. It is one of the few areas of the budget where there is widespread agreement that we need to spend more. But we also want to see that all taxpayer funds are spent carefully and effectively, and we want to help develop policies and, frankly, the public education required to protect the Nation in this new domain of warfare.

Finally, I want to offer, on behalf of the people I represent and especially on behalf of the service men and women I represent, our tremendous gratitude to General Alexander for his service to the Nation. He retires at the end of this month, and this may well be his last or one of his last hearings. General Alexander has led the National Security Agency [NSA] since 2005 and then also Cyber Command [CYBERCOM] since its creation in 2010.

These have been turbulent, challenging years, with a constant yet evolving terrorist threat and an explosion of cyber threats, as well as other national security challenges. Through it all, through terrorist plots, cyber intrusions of every description, not to mention intentional illegal disclosures of important national security information, he and the folks at NSA made sure that support for our troops in the field was a top priority. And we will never know how many of their lives were saved because of the professionalism, commitment, and focus of the people at NSA and CYBERCOM—qualities reflected in their commander.

So, General, for all your service that has meant so much to the Nation and for all your openness and candor with this and other committees in the Congress, we thank you.

I yield to the ranking member, Mr. Langevin.

STATEMENT OF HON. JAMES R. LANGEVIN, A REPRESENTATIVE FROM RHODE ISLAND, RANKING MEMBER, SUBCOMMITTEE ON INTELLIGENCE, EMERGING THREATS AND CAPABILITIES

Mr. LANGEVIN. Thank you, Mr. Chairman.

Ms. Takai, it is a pleasure to welcome you back before the subcommittee.

And, General Alexander, it is my duty to inform you that you have to endure one last go-round through the wringer before your well-earned retirement.

But we are grateful that you are both here today.

Information systems are obviously the lynchpin of everything that we do as a Nation, and the military is certainly no exception. IT continues to be a massive portion of our defense enterprise investment, and cyber operations are one of the only growth areas in the DOD budget. In today's fiscal environment, there can be no higher validation of the importance of these missions.

There is no shortage of critical discussion, of course, that we need to have this afternoon, so I am going to keep my comments pretty brief, but there are a few points I would like—that I would appreciate both of you addressing to the extent possible in your opening remarks and possibly at greater length in a classified session.

The first is the adjustments that you have made in your respective jurisdiction with regard to the gravely damaging leaks of highly classified information by Edward Snowden. To the extent possible, I know all of us would appreciate hearing how the Department has shifted to protect and prevent such insider threats in the future and especially how we are spreading those lessons learned.

And speaking of lessons learned, our recent unfortunate news about a particular IT program that was unsecured for months as a result of contract confusion raises again the complexities of contracting for IT and related services. Understanding that this is a continuing saga, I would appreciate knowing what sort of lessons are being drawn from this event and how you are working to prevent similar problems.

Also, I think the committee could also benefit from an update on the creation of the mission teams and how both of you are handling the challenges of personnel retention and growth. In particular, General, how you are using the capabilities of the Reserve Component and, Ms. Takai, how you are dealing with the increased needs and challenges stemming from the Joint Information Environment [JIE] and the cloud security model.

Given the proliferation of polymorphic malware and other advanced methodologies aimed at defeating traditional cyber defenses, I think we would be interested to know more about how the Department is defending against these threats until the Joint Information Environment comes on line.

And, as both of you know, also I am very concerned about the security of the information systems underpinning of our critical infrastructure, especially those enterprises which support the Department of Defense. I would appreciate an update on what the Department is doing to work with and better secure those networks.

And, finally, before we go into your statements and Member questions, I would just like to note for the record what an extraordinary career you have had, General Alexander. In your 40 years of service, going back to West Point, class of 1974, you have shown true dedication and commitment to America's men and women in harm's way. You have been a partner to this committee for the last 9 years, and I found your testimony always to be very candid and forthcoming.

And I am sure that certainly there were times when it would have been much easier just simply to probably just call it a career and move on to retirement, but you have persisted and accomplished truly remarkable things when it comes to investments in our cryptologic platform, standing up the Nation's first sub-unified command for cyber while fighting for the means to build our Nation's cyber force and the development—and developing the capability for our Nation to defend itself in cyberspace, all done during very turbulent and transformational times.

So, General, with that, a grateful Nation salutes you for your inspired service. I echo the comments of the chairman. And I personally wish you the very best in your retirement, in this next chapter in your life, and I hope that we will stay in touch. Thank you.

I yield back, Mr. Chairman.

Mr. THORNBERRY. Thank you.

Ms. Takai, if you would like to summarize your opening statement. And, without objection, your full statements will be made part of the record.

STATEMENT OF HON. TERESA M. TAKAI, CHIEF INFORMATION OFFICER, U.S. DEPARTMENT OF DEFENSE

Ms. TAKAI. Thank you very much. I appreciate it.

Well, first of all, Mr. Chairman and members of the subcommittee, thank you for the opportunity to be here today. It is a great honor to be here with my cyber team member. And General

Alexander and I have worked very closely, and I very much have appreciated all the support that he has provided to me and to my organization.

I would like to just touch on a few things, and I would like to perhaps answer at least some subset of the questions that were raised. I would like to give you an overview of where we are on JIE and then certainly can address a couple of the items that were discussed there. And I know we are going to talk about those more.

I would just, as an opening, mention that we are submitting and you have our fiscal year 2014 IT budget request, which is $37.7 billion. With that, we are holding our cyber investment, and our cyber investment will be $5.2 billion of that. And I think, as you know, that is a variety of both infrastructure and defense as well as other areas.

So let me just talk a minute about JIE. I think all of you know that it is really an ambitious effort to realign and restructure the way our networks are constructed, operated, and defended. And it really is there to enable U.S. Cyber Command to be able to operate and defend on our networks.

The challenge is, it is an alignment of an existing vast set of networks. It is going to change the way we assemble, configure, and use new and legacy information technologies. It is actually going to change also our operations. It will consist of enterprise-level network operation centers that will reduce the complexity and ambiguity of being able to actually see our networks. Our core data centers—as you know, we are reducing our data centers over the FYDP [Future Years Defense Program] to almost half of what we have today, and all of that within a standard single security architecture that will reduce the plethora of tools and configurations that we have.

And the ultimate beneficiary of JIE is really the commander in the field. It is also going to allow for more innovative integration of information technologies and, as a part of that, will actually help, we believe, in the question that you raised on the fit with the acquisition strategies. It will actually lay an infrastructure in place that we believe will actually help the speed of acquisition without necessarily meaning that we have to change acquisition processes per se.

Again, all of this in light of our cybersecurity program. I would just highlight a couple of other things. We are working with our defense industrial base partners on a cybersecurity information-sharing program. I highlight that because I think it is an example of what is possible from an information-sharing perspective. And General Alexander has been a continued advocate for it, and I think it does pave the way for other areas that we want to work on.

As it relates to the insider-threat question, we work very closely with USD(I) [Under Secretary of Defense for Intelligence], the intelligence organization, they're really the lead on insider threat. But I think as you have seen from some of our actions, one of my roles has been to work with them to put out policy, very closely then followed by U.S. Cyber Command putting out specific direction, in terms of reinforcing some areas, you know, like the removable media, but also reinforcing policies in terms of who is on our network.

But, ultimately, for insider threat, it is really going to be our Joint Information Environment and really tightening down, being able to see on our network but also being able to see who is there and, if in fact we have an issue, being able to catch it and contain it very quickly. So we are looking at a set of steps that is not only a single action but steps that will take place over time.

Another item that I wanted to mention is that I think there is a perception that JIE is something that is out there in the future. In fact, we are implementing elements of JIE as we go. And we will certainly talk more about our data center consolidation, our implementation of many elements of our single security architecture. And while this is going to take a period of time, I wouldn't want to leave the impression that this is all in the future and that we are not working with it and working to that right now.

A couple of other items that I would mention if, in fact, we have time to talk about them: I do have responsibility for a position navigation and timing strategy, which I think is becoming critically important, particularly as we look at it in light of potential cybersecurity threats to that area of technology. And then, finally, I think as you know, we are responsible for the Department's spectrum strategy, and there may be some questions.

So, with that, I will leave you with that summary. And, again, we appreciate the opportunity to be here.

[The prepared statement of Ms. Takai can be found in the Appendix on page 27.]

Mr. THORNBERRY. Great. Thank you.

General.

STATEMENT OF GEN KEITH B. ALEXANDER, USA, COMMANDER, UNITED STATES CYBER COMMAND

General ALEXANDER. Chairman, Ranking Member, distinguished members of the committee, it is an honor and privilege to be here for what we hope, or at least one of us hopes, is our last appearance before the committee in uniform.

I thought I would talk about two things: first, a little bit about the threat. Because I think it is important to couch what our country will face in a construct of the threat that we are going to face.

The target, exploitation, and theft of our personal data highlights some of the threats that go on in industry every day. But our Defense Department systems are scanned by adversaries about 250,000 times an hour, on average, for vulnerabilities.

And when you look at it, look at the amount of disruptive attacks, exploitations, and now destructive attacks that have hit the world. In August of 2012, Saudi Aramco was hit with one of the first destructive attacks, where the data on over 30,000 systems was destroyed. Since then, our financial networks have been hit with hundreds of disruptive distributed denial-of-service attacks, we have seen South Korea hit with destructive attacks where data was wiped off their banks, and I believe there are worse things to come.

It was interesting, out in RSA [annual cybersecurity conference], over the last couple weeks—we briefly talked about it. How bad can cyber attacks get? How about burning the internal components of a machine, whether PC or Mac, to a crisp, setting it on fire? So they actually demonstrated that out there. So that you can go all the way from disrupting to destroying the data to destroying the equipment itself.

From our perspective, there are a number of things that we have to put in place to stop this. So we came up with five key things to address this threat. And I believe we are going to have to move on on that as a Nation. And this is where, Chairman, I would really push the committee to help the Department and the rest of the government to move forward.

First, we have to get a defensible architecture. The architecture that we have, our dependence on something we call Joint Information Environment, really gets us a step in that direction.

And the reason that is so important, when you look at DOD's networks, we have 15,000 enclaves. It is very difficult to ensure that one of those doesn't get penetrated. And if they get into one, they are free to roam around all of them, and that creates a problem. Oftentimes, adversaries will get into a network and be there for a while, on the civilian side up to 9 months, before they are detected. We can't afford to have that happen in our government networks. More importantly, that is the road in for more disruptive and destructive attacks. Because once they get in, they can then do things to the network, like disrupt and destroy it.

So, a defensible architecture.

Trained and ready force. One of the good parts about Cyber Command being at NSA, I think the training of our forces is going extremely well. We have trained almost 900 people. We have 900 more, roughly, in training right now. By the end of this year, that means we will have 1,800 trained and ready personnel in teams that cover from our Cyber Protection Teams all the way up to the National Mission Force.

And those personnel from across all the services are being trained to the same standards that we set at NSA. It is important that people who operate in these networks are trained to that same standard; it is extremely important. And it is the same for the Guard and the Reserve.

So just to take that off for a minute, so the exercises that we do, CYBER FLAG and CYBER GUARD, are ways that we can hone our command and control and ensure that our teams, both in the Active and Reserve, are being trained to those standards. So one of the things we set up with the Reserve and the National Guard is to train them to just that standard and then try to set your teams up to match what the Active Component is doing.

Authorities. Here is where we need your help. We need cyber legislation. We need the ability to reach out and hear from industry when they are being attacked at network speed—the government, not just NSA and Cyber Command, but FBI [Federal Bureau of Investigation] and DHS [Department of Homeland Security]. So we have to have cyber legislation that goes beyond where the Electronic Communications Privacy Act, ECPA, and the Stored Communications Act prevent some of those sharings from going on, and we have to have that.

Command and control. We have to have the right command and control structure, seamless command and control, from the President all the way down through the SecDef [Secretary of Defense], DNI [Director of National Intelligence]; everybody understands how we are going to do this in time of crisis. That has to be set up ahead of time.

And, finally, you have to be able to see what is going on in cyberspace. If you are going to use forces to defend this Nation, they have to have a common picture of how they are going to do it. If you ask anybody to draw a diagram of what the attack looks like, get four different people, have them sit at different desks, you will get four different pictures. That means you have no coherent defense. We have to have a common picture that people can see to defend it.

Finally, I would just end by saying it has been a privilege and honor to work with Ms. Teri Takai as the DOD CIO [Chief Information Officer]. She has been a great partner, always there to help us and always helpful.

So, Chairman, thank you very much.

Thanks, Teri.

[The prepared statement of General Alexander can be found in the Appendix on page 39.]

Mr. THORNBERRY. Thank you. I appreciate the comments that both of you made.

We will go as far as we can with the questions until the votes are called. And we will do everybody on the 5-minute rule, starting now.

General Alexander, I think this is the fourth time that you have testified before this subcommittee, because we rearranged jurisdiction and concentrated cyber in one subcommittee in 2011. So just give me a rough comparison between now and 4 years ago, how the threat has changed and how our capabilities have changed. You know, which has grown the fastest—you know, just kind of a rough, for the American people, what has changed in the last 4 years on the threat and our capability.

General ALEXANDER. Chairman, I think the——

Mr. THORNBERRY. Get the microphone a little closer. Thank you.

General ALEXANDER. Or I could move up.

I think the capabilities that have changed the most are the technical capabilities for the threat to attack and for us to defend. What is lagging is the authorities.

So, to be specific, back in 2011, we pushed a memo up that said, here is what we think is going to happen, and, in fact, that did happen. So we actually were pretty close in defining the disruptive attacks that were to come. And we went to Secretary Panetta and said, here is what we think we need to do to defend against these.

I now think we need to be ready for destructive attacks. And we have tools that can be used to defend against it, but we don't have the authorities to see it, which means those tools would be useless.

Think of this as a radar system. What we have is missiles that are coming in, cyber missiles that are coming in, and no way to see where they are going, so you have no way to shoot them down. You can see them land in civilian infrastructure and say, well, we could have stopped that one if we had only seen it.

So we have to have a way of seeing so that the Defense Department, FBI, and Homeland Security can act in the interest of the Nation. That is where I think that the biggest gap is.

There are some tools and training that we are doing, but, actually, I think that is going pretty good. I think they are up—they are up where we would want them to be, in terms of being prepared to respond if authorized to do so.

Mr. THORNBERRY. Okay.

And just to be clear, when you say "destructive attack," you mean data gets destroyed or the computer literally melts down, like happened at RSA?

General ALEXANDER. Both.

Mr. THORNBERRY. Yeah. Okay.

Briefly, Ms. Takai, you talked a lot, which I appreciate, about the Joint Information Environment. One of my questions is, it has all the characteristics of a major program, yet it is a little vague on who is in charge. Who is in charge?

Ms. TAKAI. Well, sir, I can answer that. I am in charge. The Secretary has signed out two memos actually directing me to implement JIE.

Now, as part of that, though, clearly, our requirements in terms of what is necessary from JIE come from Cyber Command and the component cyber commanders to ensure that we are meeting their needs. We are taking it through our processes in the building, so it does have—and go through the Joint Staff processes to ensure that we have what we call validated requirements.

And so, while it may not be a program of record, per se—and I will come back to that—it very much is using all of the processes in the building to make sure that, again, whether it is the size and scope of DOD, we have to make sure that we have a sustained program that isn't dependent upon one person but, again, is a part of all the programs.

Let me come back to why it is not a program of record. It is not a program of record because we are not seeking to look at a funding for the program, per se. Because, largely, today, about 50 percent of our overall IT spend is in sustainment dollars, effectively in our infrastructure and what it takes for that infrastructure to move forward.

It is important that we take those moneys and direct those to the Joint Information Environment. And so, by doing that, we can ensure that we are not just adding technology, we are actually changing the underlying infrastructure.

Second thing is that it is a long-term program. It involves not only the services but all the components. And each of them has to do it within their existing architecture. They have to come up with their own implementation plans. And, in fact, that is what they have submitted to me as of this month.

Mr. THORNBERRY. Can you order a service to make a change? I mean, if you are in charge, do you have that authority?

Ms. TAKAI. Yes, sir.

Mr. THORNBERRY. If you have a validated requirement from the Joint—you can say, Air Force, Army, whoever, you do that.

Ms. TAKAI. Yes, sir.

Mr. THORNBERRY. Okay.

I want to go back to some of those legacy issues in a minute, but, at this point, I would yield back to Mr. Langevin.

Mr. LANGEVIN. Thank you, Mr. Chairman.

Along that same line, I guess, you know, I do have some concerns there, because, you know, how is the Congress and the Department, how are we expected to really have oversight visibility across this massive undertaking and, you know, the JIE, how will it interface with other ongoing initiatives?

So I want to know, will the Department provide standard programmatic guidance, such as baselines, capabilities documents, cost estimates, and schedules?

Ms. TAKAI. Yes, sir. We certainly can provide all of the underlying architecture documents, for instance, just to give you an example of the kinds of direction that we are giving to the services and the components in terms of the technical actions they are expected to take, number one.

Number two, we do have an overall plan that takes us to the point that we are today. But by about the middle of next month, I will be taking the implementation plans that are coming in from the services and creating an overall master plan. And we are more than happy to share that with the subcommittee so that you can see what our direction is. And then, on a periodic basis, we can certainly come back in and show you the status of each of the components in terms of the progress that they are making.

Mr. LANGEVIN. Okay. I think that would be important so this doesn't get away from us and we are providing the level of support that you need, as well, to make it effective.

So as the areas like electronic warfare [EW] and cyber converge, are you satisfied with your level of coordination with the EW community in the Department? And how does that coordination take place?

Ms. TAKAI. Well, sir, I am satisfied with the level of coordination, but I am—I do feel we are challenged to really keep up with being able to think through and meet the threat. That is something that we are continuing to work on.

And from an EW standpoint, I think there are a number of areas that are going to converge, in terms of what we are doing from a cybersecurity standpoint and what we are doing from a JIE perspective.

One of the things that we have just done, the Secretary has really directed me to set up a much stronger IT governance process that includes not only JIE but it includes all of the areas of technology. And one of things that we have recently done in our governance process is to restructure it. And in that restructuring, we have combined C2 [command and control] and cyber into a single governance process to try to drive the convergence that you are speaking of much closer than it is today.

Mr. LANGEVIN. Thank you.

General, do you have any thoughts on that?

General ALEXANDER. Congressman, I think the one key thing is we do see electronic warfare and cyber coming closer together technically. You can see this because of the—our wireless environment is very much akin to what you have in terms of the early-warning radars, radio direction and ranging capabilities, going digital with that, the ability to go over one link or the other, the jamming that goes on. You can actually jam, now, a distributed denial-of-service attack. You can do that in cyberspace; you can do that in EW. And I think we are going to have to push those together, because those effects are overlapping already, and we see that.

And in dealing with the services, it was our assessment in 2010 that you would start to bring all of these together into one domain. And I think we actually are going towards that and need to do that.

Mr. LANGEVIN. Probably a good segue, then, to my next question. Giving the increasing role of cyber, are you still satisfied with CYBERCOM as a sub-unified command? And what would be the benefits and drawbacks of elevation as a full combatant command, as you see them?

General ALEXANDER. So I think, as we have added on more teams, the requirement to go from sub-unified to unified is growing. And I think over the next year we have reached a tipping point where we are going to need to shift to a unified command.

In 2007, we set out a framework of four options for the Secretary of what you should/could do for building a cyber command of some sorts. It started out with a sub-unified command, went to a unified command with two options: a SOCOM [Special Operations Command]-like model or a generic COCOM [combatant command]. We believe that the SOCOM-like model is where you need to go, which gives you the training and some of the acquisition authorities over the cyber lane specifics. So it is a SOCOM-like.

And the fourth option was going to a service itself. I think it would be premature to consider doing that. I think you would really want to stop at a unified command and then say, so where to go?

Why a unified command? Command and control from the President and the Secretary directly to that commander. In cyberspace, that speed is going to be absolutely important. And I think, as we add more teams and more complexity, STRATCOM's [Strategic Command's] ability to actually play in this will continue to go down.

Now, to be completely candid, General Bob Kehler and now Admiral Haney, Cecil Haney, have been wonderful to work with. So there is no difference between us, and we both actually said the same thing at the Armed Services—the Senate Armed Services Committee hearing, as well.

Mr. LANGEVIN. Very good.

So, with that, I would yield back. I know I at least have a few seconds left.

Thank you both.

And again, General, thank you for your service, and wish you well. Thank you.

Mr. THORNBERRY. Ms. Davis.

Mrs. DAVIS. Thank you, Mr. Chairman.

And to you, General Alexander, we wish you the very best. Thank you so much for your extraordinary service.

And, Ms. Takai, thank you for being here, as well.

You know, you talked about the need for legislation and authorities. And some of that relates, of course, to the private sector and the willingness of the private sector to work together.

What problems do you see in relation to that? We obviously know there is already a history that we need to deal with. You know, what does this look like, in your estimation? What do we need to do?

General ALEXANDER. So the issue that we are wrestling with, I think, with the private sector is on two parts: How do we share data? I think that one we can actually resolve. And the next question is liability protection. And I think this is really the hard part. How do you set up the right liability protection framework? I know the Senate is actually working that one issue.

I believe you are going to have to set up some liability protection for when the government and others share, in good faith, signatures that people employ that perhaps don't act as they should have. So if I make a mistake giving industry a signature to protect them from malicious software and it also stops some other flow of traffic for a small period of time, the company that did what we asked them in good faith shouldn't be sued for that. So I think those kinds of things have to be thought through.

We have to have, though, a way for understanding when Wall Street, for example, is under attack. Right now, we get it after the fact or we get called up; it is not realtime. And, as a consequence, we can't defend them. So that is the operational requirement, from my perspective.

Mrs. DAVIS. Uh-huh. Will it take a major educational effort to do this? I guess I am trying to figure out how we get from A to B.

General ALEXANDER. Well, I think the—my understanding is the House has pushed forward a bill on that already, at least did last year, and now——

Mrs. DAVIS. Yeah.

General ALEXANDER [continuing]. The Senate needs to do the same. And I think the Senate has stated their intent to try to do that. So both the Intelligence Committee and the Armed Services Committee both have said that they want to do this. We had discussions with both of them, and all the Members say there is an imperative and a reason for doing this, we just have to go do it. They don't want to wait for something bad to happen to say, I wish we had done that last week.

Mrs. DAVIS. Right. Yeah. Okay, well, we are certainly going to be working on it, but I wondered if there is—if you have any more thoughts about, you know, really, how—I think there is so much concern in the public sector today that it makes it a little more difficult to move forward, and we all have to work on that.

Did you have a comment, Ms. Takai?

Ms. TAKAI. Yes. The one thing I would add is, again, back to some experience levels—and perhaps we can provide, you know, as this continues to unfold. I think one of the things, for instance, that we have been asked to do, in fact, as part of last year's NDAA [National Defense Authorization Act], was to begin to collect information from all of the defense industrial base, not only those that are participating in our information-sharing program.

I think that is going to start to help. I mean, we are getting a lot of concern from the defense industrial base companies today, but I think, as we roll that out, as they understand how this information is going to be used, that they see the benefit. If it is anything like the program that we are running today, we are finding that the companies, once they get into it, are very enthusiastic about it. They see what they can gain by talking to each other, not necessarily just by talking to us.

And so I know it is a small number, but, by the same token, our industrial base is fairly large. And, you know, perhaps we can use some of that information to sort of ease some of the concerns.

Mrs. DAVIS. General Alexander.

General ALEXANDER. Could I add? We have the technical ability today to apply signatures that defend the Department's networks through our systems right now that we can push out in essentially realtime. That defends us at the gateway and provides us incredible defense against evolving threats.

We see those evolving threats, we are protected. And we look over, and industry is not, and they get hit with that same threat. So by the time we get it to them, it is too late; they have already been impacted by it.

Mrs. DAVIS. Uh-huh. Yeah.

General ALEXANDER. So we have to have a way of sharing that at network speed. I think that is critical, especially when they go from exploit to disruptive attacks. We are going to have to have something like that.

Mrs. DAVIS. Thank you.

I was pleased to hear you say that the teams seem to be at least coming together in terms of the kind of training that is required. Because one of the concerns that we certainly have had in the last few years is how we really bring that kind of training to the front.

And when we look at the Guard and Reserve, how do you see that? Because we know that budget constraints are going to mean that we may not be tapping the Guard and Reserve in the same way, certainly not in terms of ground troops, perhaps. But is this an area that—really, the States can be very helpful in the Guard and Reserve, as well, but it depends on the way it moves forward. How do you see that?

General ALEXANDER. So we have sat down with NORTHCOM [Northern Command] Commander General Jacoby, with the head of the Reserves and National Guard, General Grass, Frank Grass, myself, and a number of the TAGs [The Adjutants General] and said, here is what we need to do as a starting. We have Cyber Protection Teams; here is the starting point and here is what you need for training.

We do need to leverage the Guard and Reserve, form them in the same way we are so that we can use them as we need that and train them to that same standard. The reason I think it is important is many of these have tremendous skills that we should leverage——

Mrs. DAVIS. Absolutely.

General ALEXANDER [continuing]. Especially when you look out around the country. Places like Washington and California have people with tremendous skills—and Texas, of course, and Rhode Island. I didn't want to miss those. Whew, that was close.

Mr. LANGEVIN. I am listening.

Mrs. DAVIS. Thank you.

Mr. THORNBERRY. I thank the gentlewoman. And, actually, I think we may have some further discussion on that.

Ms. Hartzler, do you have something right quick, or would you rather come back? We are down—let's see. Only about 60 people have voted, but the clock shows 4 minutes, so we can—do you want to come back?

Mrs. HARTZLER. If that is okay.

Mr. THORNBERRY. Okay.

Mrs. HARTZLER. Can I just ask——

Mr. THORNBERRY. Oh, yeah. Yeah, sure. Recognize the gentlelady.

Mrs. HARTZLER. I just came from reading the Edward Snowden report, and I am sorry I was a little late, but I wanted to finish it.

Are we going to have, are you aware of, a classified briefing just on that where I could ask specific questions following up, if you are aware?

Mr. THORNBERRY. If I could respond, this hearing is focused on Cyber Command. This subcommittee will have an intelligence briefing that will have a closed portion, where we can go deeply into the damage done to our national security, having nothing to do with NSA, that Mr. Snowden has done. So we will definitely go into more detail on that.

Mrs. HARTZLER. Yeah. I will hold my questions.

Mr. THORNBERRY. Okay, great. Thank you.

With that, if you all will excuse us, we have to run and vote. If you all will come with me, we will look for a place for you to at least try to use the phone and computer so you can make use of the time when we are away.

And, with that, the subcommittee stands in recess.

[Recess.]

Mr. THORNBERRY. The subcommittee will come back to order. And, again, let me thank everybody for their patience during that long series of votes.

Let me ask a few questions as other Members are coming back.

General Alexander, I was interested in your answer to Mr. Langevin's question about elevating Cyber Command. Admiral Jim Stavridis, retired, who is now the dean at the Fletcher School, somebody I respect a great deal, has written an article that says cyber is at a place where the Air Force was in 1947; it needs to be its own service. It is similar to SOCOM, but it is different, in that it all takes place in one domain, whereas SOCOM draws from different domains and, therefore, has to have elements from all the other services.

And so his argument is this is the new domain of warfare and we need to treat it as such, with the seriousness, with the promotion, with the dedication that we decided to do with the Air Force in 1947. What do you say to that?

General ALEXANDER. Well, I think that is one of the options that we actually looked at. I think, for the current period, for now, for the next several years, that we need to have an integrated cyber capability that goes into the services.

And the reason that I am not yet where he, Petraeus, and a couple others are is I think that, in places like Iraq, if we were to imbed cyber capabilities at the brigade level, which we will need to do, you need to have service participation in that, not a separate service as an external person coming in, but an imbedded, organic capability to that brigade itself.

So I think, as we go forward—but they need to be trained to a standard. They need to know how that force works. So it is analogous to the way the cryptologic system works. We have cryptologists who go down to the brigade who are trained to a certain level. We have them in the air, and we have them at sea. All of them are trained together and they act as one system, but they have them by service.

So I think the next correct step would be go to a unified, pause, and then see if it makes sense to take the step beyond there. And I think that kind of a deliberate approach, make sure we don't go too far and then have to collapse back.

Mr. THORNBERRY. Okay. I appreciate it.

Ms. Takai, I want to go back to some discussions you were having, I think, with Mr. Langevin. One of the things I hear from folks who are IT providers to the Department of Defense is they have to take into account all these legacy systems. And nobody else in the world, you know, has some of the systems DOD still operates, but they have to make sure that whatever they provide to DOD is compatible with or works with these legacy systems.

Everybody agrees, someday you move beyond that. But, to me, the hard question is, when do you force moving beyond the legacy systems and when do you, kind of, Band-Aid and incur the extra cost to deal with the legacy systems? How do you deal with that?

Ms. TAKAI. Well, there are two answers to that question, one of which is about the actual operation of the legacy systems, and the second, which is about the data-sharing implications of the legacy systems.

Well, one of the things that we are doing is each of the services, just by virtue of their efficiencies effort, is going through to eliminate some of these redundant legacy systems. And they have, in fact, made significant progress in cutting the number down.

But one of the things that we will be continuing to do, particularly with some of the new direction that the Secretaries directed out, in terms of my role with business systems, is to continue to reduce the number of redundant legacy systems so that we cut the complexity down.

The second piece, however, which is particularly a challenge for anyone needing to come in, is the interfaces and the need to be able to use data that is in the legacy systems, and it means you have to deal with the old technology. And one of the things that we are looking at is how to get the data from the legacy systems in a way that you can, in fact, information-share and yet not have to deal with all the old technology.

So the solution is really a combination of those two—really, those two steps forward.

Mr. THORNBERRY. Let me ask you the same question I asked you before. Can you make those things happen? If the services are dragging their feet and they say, oh, we are comfortable with this system, it is what we have always used, we don't want to go through retraining our people, can you make it happen?

Ms. TAKAI. Well, yes, sir. I have to impose some fairly draconian measures, in some cases. And we have not had to go to that point; the services are actually moving in that direction. Because, as I say, they have a challenge right now with being able to, from an IT perspective, maintain all of that technology going forward.

So, fortunately, we haven't had to go to those kinds of measures. By basically organizing and also putting the authority in the hands of all of the CIOs, including the service CIOs, we have been able to make progress.

Mr. THORNBERRY. Okay. Thank you.

Mr. Kilmer.

Mr. KILMER. Thank you, Mr. Chairman.

And thank you both for being here.

General Alexander, thanks for your service.

And, Ms. Takai, thank you and your staff. We have been in touch about a number of issues, and I sure appreciate your staff's hard work in answering our questions.

I thought I would start by asking a little bit about cloud computing. In the President's budget, he includes investments that are focused on transforming the government IT portfolio through cloud computing.

I was hoping you could speak a little bit about what DOD is doing and what NSA is doing today to expand the use of commercial cloud computing. And how are commercial cloud service providers, who are giving the ability to agencies to purchase IT services in more of a utility-based model and, thus, cutting costs significantly, being leveraged?

General ALEXANDER. Sure. So, a few years ago, NSA leveraged Google's Hadoop, MapReduce, BigTable cloud architecture and added to it a security layer and a realtime tipping and queuing capability, which is now in the openware Accumulo. So, given that, we actually have implemented that throughout much of NSA. I think that is a huge step forward.

And the reason I go to those two key points is you have to have the security layer for us to encrypt data, ensure that you protect it. All the things that we are going to talk about, insider threats and securing your data, all depend on that. And, as we go forward, it is the heart of what we would do under the Joint Information Environment. You have to have that as a security kernel, if you will, to start off.

Over to you.

Ms. TAKAI. So let me pick up from General Alexander's comments and talk about how those comments are really applicable across DOD.

First of all, we have an aggressive process to move forward on utilization of commercial cloud services. It is a part of JIE. And one of the things we are working at now is understanding how, in fact, we use commercial cloud services. So let me talk about that.

What General Alexander was talking about is the importance of ensuring that, as we move to commercial cloud providers, that they have both the ability to be secure and meet what our security requirements are; secondly, that we can operationalize them in a way that we don't lose those clouds from Cyber Command's visibility because they will be on our networks; and then, again, that from a contractual perspective, all of that is built in.

So, right now, we have four cloud providers that have been, if you will, through our security clearance. We have nine that are pending that we believe will pass that. And, I think as you know, one of the things that we work with is the Federal program, so that some of these providers will be through the Federal program; some of them will be us pushing them through the Federal program. And then we have another nine pilots of different types of services, where before we put them through the process we really want to see how they are going to operate in our environment.

The other thing that we are doing is, to General Alexander's point, is to put a model in place around security. So, for instance, in unclassified information, the bar isn't as high, if you will, to pass from a security perspective. And then when you get into classified information and then, obviously, into higher levels of classification, the bar will be a little higher. The service providers will need to actually look at the way that their cloud offering would fit within our architecture. But then they would be certified to come in and could be used by any component in DOD.

Mr. KILMER. I was hoping to ask also about cyber ranges. And, General Alexander, I was hoping you could speak to what sort of capabilities do we need to invest in for cyber ranges.

And then, also, if you could speak to, you know, is there currently a coordinating entity within the DOD to coordinate the use and policy of IT cyber ranges and test beds and systems? And if so, who is it, and how are they doing it? And if there is not, do you think that is a mission that would be best suited for CYBERCOM?

General ALEXANDER. So, if I could answer the last part of that——

Mr. KILMER. Sure.

General ALEXANDER [continuing]. First, I agree with the way you pushed that. I do think, as we get more teams, we want these teams to be trained in a joint environment. And so I do think at some point you are going to need to transition that. We have it under four different places right now. Bring them all together. And you are going to have to build the capacity to handle the number of teams that we have in an interactive way, dynamically.

So I think consolidation, going to a single provider, and growing the capacity so that you can do this in a full-up set of war games that will keep people trained. The best training, from my perspective, is really doing this on the network, actually doing it. So there is a combination of both.

I don't know if you had a chance to go out to the CYBER FLAG exercise. They actually ran a very large exercise in cyber, and I think it might be worth your while to see that so you can see where we are actually trying to take the ranges in the future.

But I do agree with the thrust of what you are saying; we need to consolidate. I actually would push it under the J–7 of Cyber

Command, as they are doing all the training, they are doing the exercises. And I think, in this case, they could also run those ranges. We just need to make sure that they are resourced for that.

Mr. KILMER. Thanks, Mr. Chairman. I yield back.

Mr. THORNBERRY. Mr. Langevin.

Mr. LANGEVIN. Thanks.

What is the average time it has taken for cloud providers to be granted approval to operate?

Ms. TAKAI. I don't know that we have an average time, but the time right now is actually in several months.

And part of the challenge there has been that, when we talk about cloud providers, they generally have a broad range of offerings. And so, even for the Federal program, in order to meet our security requirements, for instance, they have to continually monitor their cloud in order to ensure that they have all the security provisions.

They end up—that time is not so much in the approval process, but it is in the actual companies setting up to meet the security requirements that the Federal Government requires. And then, once that happens, they can be quickly certified.

Mr. LANGEVIN. Okay. Thank you.

Let me turn to another area. Are you both satisfied with your current authorities to identify, recruit, and retain qualified cyber personnel?

And, General, could you provide your assessment of how the Department is leveraging the unique ability of the Guard and Reserve to attract personnel who might otherwise be inaccessible to the Department?

I know you have talked about the Guard and Reserve and training them to the same standards and such, but being able to leverage the unique ability of the Guard and Reserve to, again, attract personnel that perhaps, you know, we wouldn't be able to afford, per se, on a long-term basis, which is obviously a challenge, I know, for us to be able to attract and retain and recruit the best and the brightest. Yet we recognize, in the Guard and Reserve, these folks are doing their day job at some very well-known and high-level IT companies, and yet they are doing their Guard and Reserve duty, and we have the ability to leverage their talents.

So if you could talk about those areas.

General ALEXANDER. So, Congressman, first, with respect to personnel, I think we need to come up with a personnel system that puts all of our cyber team in one personnel construct, especially for the NSA–CYBERCOM team.

Right now, we have the CCP [Consolidated Cryptologic Program], which covers about 85 percent; ISSP [Information System Security Program], which covers another 12, roughly, percent; then you have the MIP [Military Intelligence Program] and Air Force personnel, with another 3 percent. What this means is, when personnel actions come, you deal with four different folks. And for promotions and for raises and for everything you are dealing with, you are dealing on four different programs. You don't have an equal setting and an equal footing.

So, step one, we need to do that. That is something I have to push back to the Department, and we are doing that. I just think, as that comes forward, we would need your support on it. Because I do think, either as a test or something, it gets us to where we want to be, to have one cyber team.

This really came through on the furloughs. It was a big issue, because half the force is in, or 85 percent is in, the rest are out. Nobody wants to then go over to one of those other billets feeling they will be at risk. That is not a way to set up a team. So I think we need to fix that.

With respect to Reserve personnel, you have hit the key things. Actually, we are getting good participation, from my perspective, into the Reserves. They want to be in this area, and they are very good and very helpful. And they come from some of the best and brightest amongst industry.

The key will be getting them the training so that they have those same level of skills that the rest of the team—so if they operate in the network we don't make mistakes. And that is important, and I think we can do that.

So we are headed in the right direction. I think General Grass and others have agreed that we need to do this. I think we need to organize them the same. States will have similar requirements, so you can have them working for State things, and then when you need the Federal, we know we can employ these as teams, not as individuals. I think that will be very helpful.

Ms. TAKAI. Sir, I would just add on to speak to the civilian side, and I think General Alexander has spoken to the military side.

One of the challenges that we have on the civilian side is actually to the point—the next level of detail is really classifications and standardization of classifications for civilian employees, as well as the way that we are able to actually move them through the promotional opportunities such that they stay in the area of expertise and, you know, can continue to progress.

We are always going to have the problem with challenges of people moving outside into industry and some of the challenges with pay, but one of the things I think we need to do is to really work— DHS has put a framework together, and we are all working to it. But one of the things we need to do is to really get not only the job classifications solidified and through OPM [Office of Personnel Management], but then also to make sure that we have the right career path and we are moving people along.

Mr. LANGEVIN. Thank you.

Do you anticipate right now the additional authorities that you need to make that more seamless?

Ms. TAKAI. Well, we are pursuing that right now, sir. I couldn't tell you that we have or we have not. We are putting proposals together, certainly within DOD, for what we feel we need. And then I think both on—we are working on the civilian side, we are working with General Alexander on the military side to get that standardization. So I think that is something that we will watch it and then, if it looks like we have an issue, come back and give you an update.

Mr. LANGEVIN. And, Chairman, I had one last question if you are okay with that.

So where are your research and development [R&D] priorities over the FYDP and beyond? And what is your role in setting requirements for R&D?

General ALEXANDER. Within Cyber Command, it is on building out our infrastructure and our tools. Those are the two things that we are really doing our research and development on.

So when we say "tools," there are some sensitive things that we do, and to fully answer that I would like to show you a classified briefing, perhaps sometime when you come up, so you can see, because they have done some great things there. I think it is important to see what those tools are and what that means. It actually goes back to some of your earlier questions, and I think it would be well worth your time to see some.

Mr. LANGEVIN. Fair enough. Will do. Thank you.

Ms. TAKAI. Just to add on to what General Alexander is saying, our main priorities are not only in the defense of the network but also looking at tools around the detection of insider threat. I think that is a big area.

We actually work with AT&L [Acquisition, Technology and Logistics] on their S&T [science and technology] budget, and we co-chair the group that works with both the AT&L S&T budget but also the Investment Review Board that Mr. Kendall chairs that looks at the overall investment. Cyber Command is a part of that so that we are sure that the investment is aligned with what their priorities are.

Mr. LANGEVIN. Very good.

Well, I thank you for your answers. I thank you for the work that you all are doing.

And, General, again, congratulations. Job well done. And thank you.

I yield back.

Mr. THORNBERRY. General, I want to just go back and make sure, as we look at the administration's budget request for this year on information assurance, in the cyber environment you described—threats increasing, complexity increasing, talk about destructive, et cetera—are we spending enough money and money the right way to assure that our own networks are secure?

General ALEXANDER. This is an area that I have put forward to the Department and others that I have some concerns that we don't have adequate funding over the years, especially as we go forward in securing the networks. And there are two sets of issues that come up with that.

When we look at it, we have had to cut back across all parts of the Department, but in this area, especially, it is difficult because there aren't any service champions. The two champions happen to be Ms. Takai and I. And so the real issue comes down to, that is something that is very difficult to push forward and very hard to explain what you are buying with it. What you are buying is additional security.

So I am concerned that we don't have enough funds in those areas, and we are pushing that back to the Department. We have worked that with the USD(I), with the Department, and also to the DNI so they understand our concerns there.

Going forward, I think investment is going to have to increase in that area because of the complexity of encryption and the systems that are coming that our adversaries will have, without going into classified.

Mr. THORNBERRY. Yeah.

Ms. Takai, do you share the same concerns, at least about future years?

Ms. TAKAI. Yes, sir, I do.

I think the other item that I would add to what General Alexander is saying is that, as we are moving to the Joint Information Environment, back to your point about what do you do about legacy systems——

Mr. THORNBERRY. Uh-huh.

Ms. TAKAI [continuing]. There are times where, in fact, you can actually get more efficiency, but there are times where you need an upfront investment to do that.

So the challenge is, when we do an annual budget, it doesn't really give us an opportunity to have upfront funding in order to be able to get not only the security aspects but to be able to get the efficiencies in the later years. It is a challenge with the budgeting process, and it makes it very difficult, again, because for he and I, you know, we are pushing into the budgeting process, which is service by service today.

Mr. THORNBERRY. Yeah. Well, I would just say, for me personally, I think that is an area we want to help you with as we can. I mean, we are all constrained by these tight budgets, but it makes sense to me that sometimes you are going to have to spend more money up front to make this transition to a more secure and efficient place. But protecting our networks has got to be near the top of our list.

Okay. It wouldn't be a hearing without asking spectrum. Tell me where we are. I would hate to rob you of the opportunity to not talk about spectrum.

Ms. TAKAI. Well, sir, thank you for the opportunity.

We actually think that we are making good progress on spectrum. I think as you know, we have submitted our transition plans for the 1695 to 1710 and then also the very controversial 1755 to 1780.

I hope that the committee has been informed that we really pushed very hard for what we believe are some very innovative sharing solutions in the 1755 to 1780 in order to move it forward. And we believe that our transition plans, you know, are in discussion right now, but we believe that they will go through, so there will be that opportunity.

Going forward, thank you for the question, because I actually did bring a copy of our just newly released electromagnetic spectrum strategy that really addresses where we believe DOD needs to go in the longer term, because this isn't something that we can do in the short term.

But, lastly, we appreciate all of your support. And the last thing is, I think the challenge for us is to really figure out how to balance our growing needs for spectrum with, clearly, what the Nation's growing need is for spectrum. And I think that is going to require innovative solutions, not only on the government side, but it is also going to require innovative solutions on industry's side. And, you know, I think between the two is what is really going to bring it together.

So thank you for the question.

Mr. THORNBERRY. Yeah. Well, I hope your new long-term strategy is useful, because I do—I get the feeling a lot of times we make these decisions ad hoc, and we do need that long-term vision, because we have these competing demands from the Department and the rest of the country, and it is not a good situation to be able to just, kind of, take them one at a time.

On the spectrum you mentioned, can you meet the auction deadlines?

Ms. TAKAI. Yes, sir. They are accelerated deadlines, but we have—the team has worked very hard, and we will be able to meet the timing.

Mr. THORNBERRY. Okay.

I just had one other thing right quick.

General Alexander, in your five things, number three was authorization. And I just want to be sure I understand what sort of legal authorization you were talking about when it comes to cyber, because that is in our bailiwick.

General ALEXANDER. So the authorities——

Mr. THORNBERRY. Authorities, yeah.

General ALEXANDER. Yeah. And so the authorities really dealt with—the principal there is cyber legislation, the ability for us to deal with industry. The rest——

Mr. THORNBERRY. So you are talking about the information sharing——

General ALEXANDER. That is right.

Mr. THORNBERRY. Okay. And that is the sort of authorities.

As far as authorities related to Cyber Command's ability to defend the country in cyberspace, you feel comfortable where the legal authorities are, even though you mentioned command and control and a variety of other challenges?

General ALEXANDER. I do. I think we have the authorities within the administration, within the Department, to do what we need. Now, the question is, okay, where do we set the limits and stuff? But they are working their way through that.

Mr. THORNBERRY. Yeah. Okay. I just wanted to clarify.

Okay, great. Again, thank you all for your patience, for your work in these very important areas. And we will look forward to seeing you both again in one capacity or another.

With that, the hearing stands adjourned.

[Whereupon, at 5:35 p.m., the subcommittee was adjourned.]

APPENDIX

MARCH 12, 2014

PREPARED STATEMENTS SUBMITTED FOR THE RECORD

MARCH 12, 2014

STATEMENT BY

TERESA M. TAKAI

DEPARTMENT OF DEFENSE CHIEF INFORMATION OFFICER

BEFORE THE

HOUSE ARMED SERVICES COMMITTEE

SUBCOMMITTEE ON

INTELLIGENCE, EMERGING THREATS & CAPABILITIES

ON

"Information Technology and Cyber Operations: Modernization and Policy

Issues in a Changing National Security Environment"

March 12, 2014

Introduction

Good afternoon Mr. Chairman and distinguished Members of the Subcommittee. Thank you for this opportunity to testify before the Subcommittee today on information technology (IT) modernization and policy. I am Teri Takai, the Department's Chief Information Officer (CIO). My office is responsible for ensuring the Department has access to the information, the communication networks, and the decision support tools needed to successfully execute our warfighting and business support missions. Our mission is to ensure that these capabilities can be depended upon in the face of threats by a capable adversary in all conditions from peace to war, and particularly in the face of ever-increasing cyber threats. My focus in accomplishing these responsibilities is to ensure the effectiveness, reliability, security, and efficiency of DoD's IT capabilities for the warfighter, and ensure we are able to take advantage of future technology innovations to support the Department's missions.

I would like to give you a broad overview of the Department's IT landscape; summarize recent directions from the Secretary of Defense to strengthen the DoD CIO; and describe the Joint Information Environment (JIE), DoD's multiyear effort to restructure much of the underlying network, computing, and cyber security of the Department so as to make us more agile in deploying new decision support capabilities, make us better able to mount cyber defense of our core Department missions, and make us more efficient and better stewards of taxpayer resources. I will also briefly describe some of the activities underway in my office related to my responsibilities for overseeing Positioning, Navigation and Timing (PNT) and spectrum.

Overview of DoD's Information Technology

The Department's FY14 IT budget request was $39.6 billion and included funding for a broad variety of information technology, ranging from command and control systems, commercial satellite communications, and tactical radios to desktop computers, server computing, enterprise services like collaboration and electronic mail, and DoD business systems. These investments support mission critical operations that must be delivered both on the battlefield and in an office environment. They also provide capabilities that enable the Commander-in-Chief to communicate with and direct the military, and that support command and control, intelligence, logistics, medical and other warfighting and business support functions throughout the Department. The overall IT budget includes funding for the Department's cyber activities and efforts. These are designed to ensure that essential Department missions work well in the face of cyber attacks. These cyber efforts continue to receive the highest-level attention and support of the Department.

Secretary of Defense Organizational Review

Recently Secretary of Defense Hagel issued direction to strengthen the role of the DoD CIO. Specifically he affirmed the importance of my office as an OSD Principal Staff Assistant with the responsibilities listed above. As well, he directed actions to add functions, expand authorities, and restore stature to the DoD CIO, with a priority focus on advancing the JIE as a special interest item for the Secretary. The Secretary also directed my office to improve visibility, oversight, and governance of IT resources. And, he reaffirmed the critical importance of addressing the challenges posed by cybersecurity.

My office has completed the development of a plan of action and milestones to implement the Secretary's direction. We are taking actions necessary to increase visibility into IT budgets and spending patterns, and are strengthening our analysis of IT investments and evolving our processes for IT governance and oversight.

Consistent with the Secretary's direction, my office is working closely with others in the Department to identify ways to adapt our existing processes to ensure adaptability to technological advances and ability to defend the network against emerging cybersecurity threats. In particular, we are examining how best to leverage the Department's three core processes - requirements, budgeting, and acquisition - to address the systemic conditions resulting in DoD's stove-piped IT infrastructure. This is critical if we are to achieve the agility and responsiveness from IT systems that warfighters both demand and deserve, and improve our ability to defend against cyber attacks. My office is working closely with the offices of the Under Secretary of Defense for Acquisition, Technology and Logistics (USD(AT&L)), Deputy Chief Management Officer (DCMO) and others to make the existing acquisition process more flexible and agile for IT and IT services, while ensuring compliance with enterprise standards.

Joint Information Environment
Mission success depends upon the ability of our military commanders and civilian leaders to act decisively based on the most timely and accurate data and information. Recognizing that information is a strategic asset, DoD is undertaking an ambitious effort to re-align and restructure how our many IT networks are constructed, operated and defended in order to provide better information access to the user, improve our ability to not only defend the networks and the data, but make it responsive to constantly changing technological and operational factors. The challenge is amplified because capable adversaries are extremely active in seeking to penetrate DoD systems, compromise command and control, to steal or destroy sensitive and strategic information, to gain an upper hand on U.S. forces and warfighting capability. Consequently, DoD is pursuing the alignment of existing vast IT networks into a Joint Information Environment (JIE) construct. First and foremost, JIE will improve mission effectiveness. It is intended to enable and empower our military's decisive edge-our people-by providing warfighters and our mission partners a shared IT infrastructure consisting of federated networks with common configurations and management, and a common set of enterprise services, within a single security architecture.

The JIE will change the way we assemble, configure, and use new and legacy information technologies. It will consist of enterprise level network operations centers that will reduce the complexity and ambiguity of seeing and controlling the numerous networks within DoD; a set of core data centers - significantly reducing the current number of DoD data centers while ensuring the information is secured and available where needed; and standard, single security architecture that will reduce the number of organizationally owned firewalls, unique routing algorithms, and inefficient routing of information that currently exists today. Together with the single, authoritative identity management and access control, emerging cloud capability, mobile computing devices and data-focused applications, and common IT enterprise services, JIE will provide the information environment to flexibly create, store, disseminate, and access data, applications, and other computing services when and where needed. It will better protect the integrity of information from unauthorized access while increasing the ability to respond to security breaches across the system as a whole.

The ultimate beneficiary of JIE is the commander in the field, allowing for more innovative integration of information technologies, operations, and cyber security at a tempo more appropriate to today's fast-paced operational conditions. Specific benefits include:

- A standardized information and security architecture across software, servers, the network, mobile and fixed user computing, and identity and access control systems. Users and systems will be able to trust their connection from end to end with the assurance that the information and systems involved in a mission are correct and working even during a cyber attack. The JIE architecture will enable cyber operators at every level to see the status of the networks for operations and security and will provide standard resilience and cyber maneuver options for all cyber forces. This will minimize complexity for a synchronized cyber response, maximize operational efficiencies, and reduce risk. Most importantly, unlike the one size fits all networks the department has now, the JIE will provide mission commanders more freedom to take operational risk with the networks since the risks can be contained to the decision support and systems specifically needed for that mission.

- Consolidation of data centers, operations centers and help desks will enable users and systems to have timely and secure access to the data and services needed to accomplish their assigned missions, regardless of their location.

- A consistent DoD-wide IT architecture that defines enterprise standards and supports effective fielding of Department capabilities in support of information sharing, as well as sustainment and integration of legacy systems.

The Department plans on utilizing the Services existing programs, initiatives, and technical refresh to deploy or migrate to JIE standards utilizing specific implementation guidance.

Data Center Consolidation. An important aspect within JIE is the active consolidation of the Department's numerous data centers. The Department's efforts are consistent with and support the Federal Data Center Consolidation Initiative (FDCCI) being led by the Federal CIO, and have resulted in the closure of 277 data centers as of first quarter FY14. The Department's progress in this area has been aided by Section 2867 of the FY12 National Defense Authorization Act.

The Department has established four classes of data centers to assist in the development and execution of our data center consolidation strategy. These four types of data centers are:

- Core Data Center (CDC) - delivers enterprise services and provides primary migration point for systems and applications; these are our most important data centers, strategically located to provide speed of access to global information requirements;

- Installation Processing Node (IPN) - provides local services to DoD installations and hosting systems not suited for CDCs; these will be located at the installation level, and will consolidate the duplicative data centers at the installations;

- Special Purpose Processing Node (SPPN) - provides compute and storage for fixed infrastructure or facilities, such as test ranges, labs, medical diagnostic equipment, and machine shops; and

- Tactical/Mobile Processing Node (TPN) - provides support to the deployed warfighter at the tactical edge; these unique "data centers" directly support the warfighter in a disadvantaged or tactical environment, but connect back into the Generating Force information sources and core data centers.

Cloud Computing. Cloud Computing is becoming a critical component of the JIE and the Department's IT modernization efforts and will enable users the access to data anywhere, anytime on any approved device. One key objective is to drive the delivery and adoption of a secure, dependable, resilient multi-provider enterprise cloud computing environment that will enhance mission effectiveness and improve IT efficiencies. Cloud services will enhance warfighter mobility by providing secure access to mission data and enterprise services regardless of where the user is located and what device he or she uses.

My office continues to investigate new ways to leverage commercial cloud computing innovations and efficiencies to improve the Department. The nature of the Department's mission, and the risk to national security if DoD information were to be compromised, requires the careful evaluation of commercial cloud services, especially in areas of cybersecurity, continuity of operations, and resilience. To improve our cybersecurity posture with regards to commercial cloud computing, we are participating in the Federal Risk Authorization and Management Program (FedRAMP) and updating our own cybersecurity policies.

There are two key components of the Department's cloud strategy. The first component is the establishment of a private enterprise cloud infrastructure that supports the full range of DoD activities in unclassified and classified environments. The second is the Department's adoption of commercial cloud services that can meet the Departments cybersecurity needs while providing capabilities that are at least as effective and efficient as those provided internally.

Enterprise Services. As previously noted, enterprise services are those global applications that can be used by many, if not all users within DoD. They are a key element of achieving more effective operations and improved security across the Department. An example of this is Defense Enterprise Email, which is an enterprise messaging tool, built by consolidating existing disparate email servers into a global capable server and operated by the Defense Information Systems Agency (DISA) on a fee-for-service basis. The result is a common DoD enterprise email and contact address list and consolidated email service.

The basis for enterprise email and other services is an authoritative identity service. Defense Enterprise Email is currently used by DISA, the US Army, the Joint Staff, the Office of the Secretary of Defense, Defense Manpower Data Center, Office of Naval Research, Navy Recruiting Command, HQ Air Force, Air Force District Washington, EUCOM, SOUTHCOM, TRANSCOM, AFRICOM and USFJ. As of February 2014, there are 1.6 million enterprise email users on the Department's unclassified network and 150,000 users on the DoD Secret network. Continued adoption and consolidation to this capability is progressing.

Cybersecurity

Cybersecurity is one of the highest priorities of the Administration and the Department. The primary cybersecurity goal of my office is ensuring that essential DoD missions are dependable and resilient in the face of cyber exploits and attacks by a capable adversary. This is also a primary concern driving the other improvement efforts, particularly JIE. This focus on mission assurance, rather than on computer or system security, is one of the primary changes in the department's cybersecurity approach. This approach enables us to move from an approach of bolting on cyber security solutions to one where resilient, mission assurance and cyber security characteristics will be built into the total information environment.

JIE gives certain operational commanders more freedom to take operational cyber security risks. We accomplish this by using "risk zones" in the design of the JIE computing and networks; these zones help keep the risks assumed by a particular mission from spilling over into other missions. This is also a significant change from today's DoD networks which impose more operational constraints on commanders. Other primary cybersecurity goals include improved safe sharing with whatever partners a mission requires, and a continued need to keep a secret. Through refinement of the JIE concept, including the JIE single security architecture, we have concluded that all of these cyber security goals can be achieved, and the Department will have better joint warfighting decision support, better operational and acquisition agility, and better efficiency.

Like other IT efforts, cybersecurity is a team sport within the department, and these efforts span many organizations. In particular, I work closely with General Alexander at U.S. Cyber Command, and others in the Office of the Secretary of Defense, the Military Departments and Defense Agencies to ensure cybersecurity issues are being addressed.

Single Security Architecture (SSA). A key priority in the last year has been the development of a unifying, joint cybersecurity approach for the design of the JIE. This is the JIE Single Security Architecture (SSA). Although many of the DoD's cyber security initiatives are common across all DoD organizations, each military service has had the ability to make important decisions about how to design computing and networks and about how to structure cyber defenses. This has led to several challenges, such as diversity in the cybersecurity protections of the DoD that does not provide a common level of protection for joint missions (because the IT for these missions is designed and operated by many organizations), and sometimes interferes with the collaborative attack detection, diagnosis, and reaction so necessary in a complex organization like DoD . Finally, the challenge caused by this diversity can interfere with a joint commander's ability to share information with external mission partners.

To solve these problems, the SSA provides for a common approach to the structure and defense of computing and the networks across all DoD organizations. This engineering of the cyber security approach "end-to-end" will significantly improve DoD's ability to resist cyber-attacks; to dampen the spread of successful attacks; and to detect, diagnose, and react to attacks in ways that are optimized for joint missions. Owing to the standardization and cyber data sharing of JIE, cyber defenders will have broad visibility into the computing and networks, and via secure remote management and automation, they will be able to much more quickly construct and execute defensive actions. In addition, the risk containment zones the SSA defines in the server computing and the network will enable joint commanders to better contain cyber risk to mission while sharing as broadly with external partners as a mission requires. It will also make development of new decision support capabilities simpler and easier since many program offices will not need to worry about most cybersecurity protections, but will instead be able to build software applications on top of the standard protections and situational awareness capabilities provided by JIE.

The Defense Industrial Base (DIB) Cybersecurity (CS) /Information Assurance (IA) Program. The DoD's DIBCS/IA Program, overseen by my office, is a successful public/private cyber information sharing program that is a model for other government/industry cybersecurity efforts. The program provides two-way cyber information sharing to include classified threat information sharing by the government, with voluntary sharing of incident data by industry, as well as sharing of mitigation and remediation strategies, digital forensic analysis, and cyber intrusion damage assessments.

As an example, the DoD provides fast analysis of malicious software reported by industry and quickly shares with the DIB CS/IA participants, and with the rest of the Federal Government, machine readable indicators of the attack that can very quickly be deployed to protect others against new and emerging threats detected by any of the participating companies. While threats cannot be eliminated, the DIB CS/IA program enhances each DIB participant's capabilities to mitigate the risk, thereby further safeguarding DoD information that resides on, or that transits, DIB unclassified networks.

Building on this successful model, the DoD partnered with the Department of Homeland Security to put in place a means of using even more highly classified information to protect the networks of participating companies. Under the DIB Enhanced Cybersecurity Services (DECS) program, the government provides highly classified cyber threat information either directly to a DIB company or to the DIB company's Commercial Service Provider (CSP). This sensitive, government-furnished information enables these DIB companies, or the CSPs on behalf of their DIB customers, to counter additional types of malicious cyber activity. The CSPs provide the protections as a commercial fee-for-service offering, so the government is not involved in the financial aspects of the transaction between a CSP and the participating DIB company.

DoD is the government point of contact for the participating DIB companies, through the DoD's DIB CS/IA Program. DHS is the government point of contact for participating CSPs, under the umbrella of DHS' Enhanced Cybersecurity Services program, a broader effort to protect U.S. critical infrastructure

Insider Threat. The threat that insiders will use their authorized access to do harm to the security of the United States has long been recognized by the DoD. This threat can include damage to the United States through espionage, terrorism, or unauthorized disclosure of information, or through the loss or degradation of departmental resources or capabilities, including acts of violence against our greatest asset, our personnel. Information is one of the greatest sources of power, and it must be appropriately protected, with access to our most sensitive information restricted to those with a real "need to know", while still enabling sharing as warranted.

In consideration of damage from disclosures of classified information stolen by insiders, including the WikiLeaks and the more recent unauthorized disclosures, the Department has conducted extensive reviews of its posture, and the Secretary has directed corrective measures be undertaken.

Last year the Under Secretary of Defense for Intelligence (USD(I)) and I released a joint memorandum directing an initial program of required actions and procedures to strengthen our insider threat safeguards. These measures included:

- the revalidation of the need for Privileged Access and the suitability of each person in a Privileged Role (e.g. system administrators) to minimize their numbers to those absolutely required for the mission;
- stronger safeguards on the use of Removable Media, including two person controls for their use in Sensitive Compartmentalized Information Facilities (SCIFs); and
- direction to complete implementation of our Public Key Infrastructure (PKI) efforts. The Department has made excellent progress on these efforts, but we must continue to strengthen our cybersecurity measures.

We have worked with the White House's Senior Information Sharing and Safeguarding Steering Committee to develop further safeguarding measures to mitigate the risks to our most sensitive information. We are about to issue direction to implement these measures, which include tasks to enhance the security culture, improve business practices, reduce the risks associated with "privileged" users, and improve personnel security through Continuous Evaluation.

In all these efforts, we have been working to ensure a comprehensive Department-response. We work closely with USD(I), the Department's lead for Insider Threat, on the Department's plan for an Insider Threat program; with U.S. Cyber Command as we develop further insider threat mitigation strategies for our networks, and with DISA as we evaluate and develop technical solutions.

DoD Strategy for Defending Networks, Systems, and Data. The DoD CIO published a new Strategy for Defending Networks, Systems, and Data in October 2013. The strategy identifies strategic imperatives to ensure the protection, integrity, and assurance of DoD cyber assets. It is focused in four key areas: establishing a Resilient Cyber Defense Posture; Transform Cyber Defense Operations; Enhance Cyber Situational Awareness; and Assure Survivability against Highly Sophisticated Cyber Attacks. In the near term, we will be finalizing the Implementation Plan for the strategy. To ensure success going forward, we will collaborate closely with others in the Department.

Cyberspace Workforce and IT Acquisition Workforce Development.
A critical component of readiness is a workforce that is properly sized, well trained and equipped. In concert with the Department's JIE transformation, the DoD is implementing a comprehensive strategy to transform legacy and evolving workforces such as IT, information assurance (IA), and cyber mission teams into a cohesive cyberspace workforce. The DoD cyberspace workforce strategy focuses on recruiting, training, and retaining the necessary workforce to build and operate its networks as well as defend U.S. national interests in cyberspace. This community will ensure that the DoD can acquire, structure, operate and defend its information, networks, systems, services and capabilities to achieve operational and strategic advantage in cyberspace. To be successful, it will need to expand learning opportunities from traditional classroom training to include a variety of training environments, including virtual and mobile training; hands-on laboratories; leveraging cyber ranges and focusing on both individual and team cyber skills development in a realistic environment.

The Department is leveraging established training and education venues both internally and externally to maximize professional development opportunities for the cyberspace workforce, and identifying where gaps exist in training and education programs. One new initiative is our collaboration with the Joint Staff and the National Defense University on a cyber-centric Joint Professional Military Education program to educate military and civilian leaders on key cyberspace tenets.

With regard to the IT acquisition workforce specifically, we are collaborating with the USD(AT&L) to strengthen the IT acquisition workforce, with emphasis on improving cybersecurity capabilities. Two years ago, the Under Secretary and I co-signed a strategic plan for the IT Acquisition Workforce which has served as the springboard for a series of ongoing initiatives. These efforts include conducting a comprehensive review and update of the Defense Acquisition University's (DAU) IT acquisition curriculum, and removing roadblocks to training and certification, enabling the Department to achieve a 20 percentage point increase in the certification rate of qualified personnel.

In all of our development efforts, we are collaborating with other acquisition career fields (particularly program management, engineering, contracting, and test and evaluation) and are also working with Acquisition leadership to infuse cybersecurity training across all DAU academic disciplines in recognition of the critical roles many acquisition personnel perform within the cyberspace workforce. Initiatives include collaborating with AT&L on a Cybersecurity Handbook for Program Managers, in draft, to provide program managers clear and concise guidance on what cybersecurity activities should be conducted at each point in the acquisition process. We are also leading a cross-functional working group in the development of a cybersecurity distance learning course to provide foundational insight on critical cybersecurity issues across the acquisition lifecycle. The goal is to ensure the Department follows an integrated, holistic approach to cybersecurity in the design, development, deployment and sustainment of all our programs, irrespective of one's particular career field. These initiatives, as well as Service-specific efforts will ensure that, together, DoD is creating a robust training and education environment to sustain a world class, mission ready cyberspace workforce. However, today's budget constrained environment limits the speed at which the Department can implement the changes needed to evolve and meet the demands of the cyberspace domain.

Space-based positioning, navigation and timing (PNT) and Spectrum

In addition to my responsibilities for IT and cybersecurity, I am also the Secretary's principal staff assistant for several other critical information capabilities, including PNT and spectrum.

PNT provides crucial capability to military, civil, and commercial users worldwide. We are working to better integrate the services of the Global Positioning System (GPS) as the primary means of delivering PNT which provides our nation and allies the ability to precisely navigate anywhere in the world. Our PNT architecture provides our nation and allies precise target location, the ability to strike with a minimum of collateral damage, navigation capabilities that support logistics, command and control, and friendly force tracking, and precise timing. This latter feature is critical to encryption, synchronization and integration of data networks within the communications and cyber enterprises. With this understanding, we are working, as a high priority, several infrastructure upgrades to protect this critical piece of cyber terrain.

Spectrum has become increasingly important not only to the Department's missions, but to consumers and the economy of the nation as a whole. The use of the electromagnetic spectrum continues to be a critical enabler of our warfighting capabilities and the Department's cyber operations. Defense leadership is cognizant and sensitive to the unprecedented spectrum demands resulting from the Department's increasing reliance on spectrum-dependent technologies and the rapid modernization of commercial mobile devices. Fully recognizing the linkages between national security and economic prosperity, the DoD is fully committed to the President's 500 MHz initiative to make spectrum available for commercial broadband use, the implementation of more effective and efficient use of this finite radio-frequency spectrum and the development of solutions to meet these goals while ensuring national security and other federal capabilities are preserved.

To that end, the Department has developed a plan that will make 25MHz of spectrum available to commercial industry on a shared basis, thus achieving a balance between expanding wireless and broadband capabilities for the nation and the need for access to support warfighting capabilities in support of our national security.

Conclusion

Maintaining information dominance for the warfighter is critical to our national security. The efforts outlined above will ensure that the Department's information capabilities provide better mission effectiveness and security, and are delivered in a manner that makes the most efficient use of financial resources. I ask that you strongly support, authorize, and fund the Department's key cybersecurity and Information Technology modernization programs. I want to thank you for your interest.

Teresa M. Takai

Chief Information Officer

Teri Takai is the Department of Defense Chief Information Officer (DoD CIO). She serves as the principal advisor to the Secretary of Defense for Information Management/Information Technology and Information Assurance as well as non-intelligence Space systems, critical satellite communications, navigation, and timing programs, spectrum and telecommunications. She provides strategy, leadership, and guidance to create a unified information management and technology vision for the Department and to ensure the delivery of information technology based capabilities required to support the broad set of Department missions.

Ms. Takai previously served as Chief Information Officer for the State of California. As a member of the Governor's cabinet, she advised the governor on the strategic management and direction of information technology resources as the state worked to modernize and transform the way California does business with its citizens.

As California's CIO, Ms. Takai led more than 130 CIOs and 10,000 IT employees spread across the state's different agencies, departments, boards, commissions and offices. During her tenure as State CIO, Teri pursued an agenda that supports viewing California's IT operations from an enterprise perspective, including: Forming a Project Management and Policy Office, release of the California Information Technology Strategic Plan, passage of the Governor's IT Reorganization Proposal, establishing a Capital Planning Process and directing agency consolidation activities.

Prior to her appointment in California, Ms. Takai served as Director of the Michigan Department of Information Technology (MDIT) since 2003, where she also served as the state's Chief Information Officer. In this position, she restructured and consolidated Michigan's resources by merging the state's information technology into one centralized department to service 19 agencies. Additionally, during her tenure at the MDIT, Ms. Takai led the state to being ranked number one four years in a row in digital government by the Center for Digital Government. Additionally, in 2005, Ms. Takai was named "Public Official of the Year" by Governing magazine. She is also Past-President of the National Association of State Chief Information Officers and currently serves on the Harvard Policy Group on Network-Enabled Services and Government.

Before serving in state government, Ms. Takai worked for the Ford Motor Company for 30 years, where she led the development of the company's information technology strategic plan. She also held positions in technology at EDS and Federal-Mogul Corporation. Ms. Takai earned a Master of Arts degree in management and a Bachelor of Arts degree in mathematics from the University of Michigan.

UNCLASSIFIED

STATEMENT OF

GENERAL KEITH B. ALEXANDER

COMMANDER

UNITED STATES CYBER COMMAND

BEFORE THE

HOUSE COMMITTEE ON ARMED SERVICES

SUBCOMMITTEE ON INTELLIGENCE, EMERGING THREATS

AND CAPABILITIES

12 MARCH 2014

Chairman Thornberry, Ranking Member Langevin, and distinguished members of the Committee, thank you for the opportunity to speak to you today on behalf of the men and women of the United States Cyber Command (USCYBERCOM). As you know, this will be the last time I have the honor of talking about our Command's fine and dedicated Service members and civilian personnel before this Committee. It always gives me great pleasure to tell you about their accomplishments, and I am both grateful for and humbled by the opportunity I have been given to lead them in the groundbreaking work they have done in defense of our nation.

USCYBERCOM is a subunified command of U.S. Strategic Command in Omaha, Nebraska though based at Fort Meade, Maryland. It has approximately 1,100 people (military, civilians, and contractors) assigned with a Congressionally-appropriated budget for Fiscal Year 2014 of approximately $562 million in Operations and Maintenance (O&M), Research, Development, Test and Evaluation (RDT&E), and military construction (MILCON). USCYBERCOM also has key Service cyber components: Army Cyber Command/Second Army, Marine Forces Cyberspace Command, Fleet Cyber Command/Tenth Fleet, and Air Forces Cyber/24th Air Force. Together they are responsible for directing the defense ensuring the operation of the Department of Defense's information networks, and helping to ensure freedom of action for the United States military and its allies—and, when directed, for defending the nation against attacks in cyberspace. On a daily basis, they are keeping U.S. military networks secure, supporting the protection of our nation's critical infrastructure from cyber attacks, assisting our combatant commanders, and working with other U.S. Government agencies tasked with defending our nation's interests in cyberspace.

USCYBERCOM resides with some key mission partners. Foremost is the National Security Agency and its affiliated Central Security Service (NSA/CSS). The President's recent decision to maintain the "dual-hat" arrangement under which the Commander of USCYBERCOM also serves as the Director of NSA/Chief, CSS means the co-location of USCYBERCOM and NSA/CSS will continue to benefit our nation. NSA/CSS has unparalleled capabilities for detecting threats in foreign cyberspace, attributing cyber actions and malware, and guarding national security information systems. At USCYBERCOM, we understand that re-creating a mirror capability for the military would not make operational or fiscal sense. The best, and only, way to meet our nation's needs today, to bring the military cyber force to life, and to exercise good stewardship of our nation's resources is to leverage the capabilities (both human and technological) that have been painstakingly built up at Fort Meade. Our nation has neither the resources nor the time to redevelop from scratch the capability that we gain now by working with our co-located NSA partners. Let me also mention our other key mission partner and neighbor at Fort Meade, the Defense Information Systems Agency (DISA). DISA is vital to the communications and the efficiency of the entire Department, and its people operate in conjunction with us at USCYBERCOM on a constant basis. We all work in conjunction with the extensive efforts of several federal government mission partners, particularly the Department of Homeland Security (DHS), the Department of Justice and its Federal Bureau of Investigation (FBI), and other departments and agencies. We also work with private industry and allies in the overall mission of securing our networks, identifying threat actors and intentions, building resiliency for federal and critical infrastructure systems, and supporting law enforcement in investigating the theft and manipulation of data.

Allow me to review the highlights since our last posture hearing before the Committee a year ago. The main point I want to leave with you is that we in US Cyber Command, with the Services and other partners, are doing something that our military has never done before. We are putting in place foundational systems and processes for organizing, training, equipping, and operating our military cyber capabilities to meet cyber threats. USCYBERCOM and the Services are building a world class, professional, and highly capable force in readiness to conduct full spectrum cyberspace operations. Seventeen out of one hundred thirty-three projected teams have achieved full or "initial" operational capability, and those teams are already engaged in operations and accomplishing high-value missions. The Cyber Mission Force is no longer an idea on a set of briefing slides; its personnel are flesh-and-blood Soldiers, Marines, Sailors, Airmen, and Coast Guardsmen, arranged in military units that are on point in cyberspace right now. We are transforming potential capability into a reliable source of options for our decision makers to employ in defending our nation. Future progress in doing so, of course, will depend on our ability to field sufficient trained, certified, and ready forces with the right tools and networks to fulfill the growing cyber requirements of national leaders and joint military commanders. That is where we need your continued support.

The Threat Picture

The Department of Defense along with the Department of Homeland Security, the Department of Justice, and the Federal Bureau of Investigation have primary responsibilities to defend the United States in cyberspace and to operate in a global and rapidly evolving field. Our economy, society, government, and military all depend on assured security and reliability in this man-made space, not only for communications and data storage, but also for the vital synchronization of actions and functions that underpins our defenses and our very way of life. USCYBERCOM concentrates its efforts on defending military networks and watching those actors who possess the capability to harm our nation's interests in cyberspace or who intend to prepare cyber means that could inflict harm on us in other ways.

Unfortunately, the roster of actors who concern us is long, as is the sophistication of the ways they can affect our operations and security. We have described some of these in previous hearings, and I know the Director of National Intelligence recently opened his annual World Wide Threat Assessment for Congress with several pages on cyber threats, so I'll be brief here.

I can summarize what is happening by saying that the level and variety of challenges to our nation's security in cyberspace differs somewhat from what we saw and expected when I arrived at Fort Meade in 2005. At that time many people, in my opinion, regarded cyber operations as the virtual equivalents of either nuclear exchanges or commando raids. What we did not wholly envision were the sort of cyber campaigns we have seen in recent years. Intruders today seek persistent presences on military, government, and private networks (for the purposes of exploitation and disruption). These intruders have to be located, blocked, and extracted over days, weeks, or even months. Our notion of cyber forces in 2005 did not expect this continuous, persistent engagement, and we have since learned the extent of the resources required to wage such campaigns, the planning and intelligence that are essential to their success, and the degree of collaboration and synchronization required across the government and with our allies and international partners. Through concerted efforts, and with a bit of luck, we are creating capabilities that are agile enough to adapt to these uses and others, and I am convinced we have found a force model that will give useful service as we continue to learn and improvise for years to come.

We have some key capability gaps in dealing with these increasingly capable threats. Cyberspace is a medium that seems more hospitable to attackers than defenders, and compared to what real and potential adversaries can do to harm us, our legacy information architecture and some of our weapons systems are not as "cyber robust" as they need to be. Our legacy forces lack the training and the readiness to confront advanced threats in cyberspace. Our commanders do not always know when they are accepting risk from cyber vulnerabilities, and cannot gain reliable situational awareness, neither globally nor in US military systems. In addition, the authorities for those commanders to act have been diffused across our military and the US government, and the operating concepts by which they could act are somewhat undefined and not wholly realistic. Further our communications systems are vulnerable to attacks. We need to rapidly pursue a defense in depth as we envision with the fielding of the Joint Information Environment.

These gaps have left us at risk across all the USCYBERCOM mission areas that I described above.

USCYBERCOM's Priorities

USCYBERCOM is addressing these gaps by building cyber capabilities to be employed by senior decisionmakers and Combatant Commanders. In accordance with the Department of Defense's *Strategy for Operating in Cyberspace*, the people of USCYBERCOM (with their NSA/CSS counterparts) are together assisting the Department in building:

1) A defensible architecture;
2) Trained and ready cyber forces;
3) Global situational awareness and a common operating picture;
4) Authorities that enable action;
5) Concepts for operating in cyberspace;

We are finding that our progress in each of these five areas benefits our efforts in the rest. We are also finding the converse—that a lack of momentum in one area can result in slower progress in others. I shall discuss each of these priorities in turn.

Defensible Architecture: The Department of Defense (DoD) owns seven million networked devices and thousands of enclaves. USCYBERCOM, with its Service cyber components, NSA/CSS, and DISA, monitors the functioning of DoD networks, providing the situational awareness to enable dynamic defenses. Unfortunately, DoD's current architecture in its present state is not fully defensible. That is why the Department is building the DoD Joint Information Environment (JIE), comprising a shared infrastructure, enterprise services, and a single security architecture to improve mission effectiveness, increase security, and realize IT efficiencies. The JIE, together with the cyber protection teams that I shall describe in a moment, will give our leaders the ability to truly defend our data and systems. Senior officers from USCYBERCOM and DISA serve on JIE councils and working groups, and together with leaders from the office of the DoD's Chief Information Officer, Joint Staff J6, and other agencies, are guiding the JIE's implementation (with NSA's support as Security Adviser). JIE has been one of my highest priorities as Commander, USCYBERCOM and Director, NSA/CSS.

Trained and Ready Forces: Over the last year we have made great progress in building out our joint cyber force. When I spoke to you in March 2013 we had just begun to establish the Cyber Mission Forces in the Services to present to USCYBERCOM. This force has three main aspects: 1) Cyber National Mission Teams to help defend the nation against a strategic cyber attack on our critical infrastructure and key resources; 2) Cyber Combat Mission Teams under the direction of the regional and functional Combatant Commanders to support their objectives; and 3) Cyber Protection Teams to help defend DoD information environment and our key military cyber terrain. On January 17, 2014 we officially activated the Cyber National Mission Force – the U.S. military's first joint tactical command with a dedicated mission focused on cyberspace operations. We have plans to create 133 cyber mission teams by the end of FY 2016, with the majority supporting the Combatant Commands and the remainder going to USCYBERCOM to support national missions. The teams will work together with regional and functional commanders according to a command and control construct that we are actively helping to forge and field.

The training for this force is happening now on two levels. At the team level, each cyber mission team must be trained to adhere to strict joint operating standards. This rigorous and deliberate training process is essential; it ensures the teams can be on-line without jeopardizing vital military, diplomatic, or intelligence interests. Such standards are also crucial to assuring intelligence oversight and to securing the trust of the American public that military operations in cyberspace do not infringe on the privacy and civil liberties of U.S. persons. Our training system is in the midst of certifying thousands of our people to high and joint military-wide standards.

At the individual level, we are using every element of capacity in our Service schools and in NSA to instruct members of the Cyber Mission Force teams. We have compiled a training and readiness manual, a "summer school" for cyber staff officers, and are shaping professional military education to enhance the cyber savvy of the force. To save time and space, furthermore, we have established equivalency standards to give individuals credit for training they have already taken in their Services and at NSA, with a board to adjudicate how much credit to confer for each course. Finally, we have established Job Qualification Records for team work roles to provide joint standards, further reinforcing common baselines of knowledge, skills and abilities across Service-component teams.

As our training system geared up to meet our need for trained operators and certified teams, sequestration-level reductions and furloughs last year seriously impeded our momentum. The uncertain budget situation complicated our training efforts; indeed, we had to send people home in the middle of our first-ever command and staff course last summer. Moreover, every day of training lost had cascading effects for the overall force development schedule, delaying classes, then courses, and then team certifications, to the point we are about six months behind where we had planned to be in training our teams. We are only now catching up to where we should have been months ago in building the Cyber Mission Force.

Increased Operational Awareness: Enhanced intelligence and situational awareness in our networks help us know what is happening in cyberspace. Our goal is to build a common operating picture, not only for the cyber activities of organizations based at Fort Meade but also across the U.S. government. We are moving toward this objective, for instance by coordinating the activities of the USCYBERCOM and NSA operations centers. Achieving it should let all who secure and defend our networks synchronize their activities, as well as see how adversarial and defensive actions can affect one another, which in turn enhances the efforts of planners and the predictability of the effects they seek to attain.

Capacity to Take Action: The last year saw increased collaboration between defenders and operators across the US government and with private and international partners. USCYBERCOM played important roles in several areas. USCYBERCOM, for instance, has been integrated in the government-wide processes for National Event responses. This regularly exercised capability will help ensure that a cyber incident of national significance can elicit a fast and effective response at the right decisionmaking level, to include pre-designated authorities and self-defense actions where necessary and appropriate. In addition, USCYBERCOM participated in whole-of-government actions with partners like the Departments of State, Justice, and Homeland Security in working against nation-state sponsored cyber exploitation and distributed denial-of-service attacks against American companies. Finally, we already benefit from sharing information on cyber threats with the services and agencies of key partners and allies, and are hopeful that cybersecurity legislation will one day make it easier for the U.S. Government and the private sector to share threat data in line with what the Administration has previously requested.

Operating Concepts: To oversee and direct the nation's cyber forces, as previously mentioned, we have established a National Mission Force Headquarters in USCYBERCOM at Fort Meade. This functions in parallel with analogous headquarters units (the four Joint Force Headquarters) for the Service cyber components, which themselves work with the NSA/CSS regional operating centers in Georgia, Texas, and Hawaii.

We can report some good news with respect to the realism of our cyber exercises, which put these operating concepts to the test. USCYBERCOM regularly participates in more than twenty Tier 1 Combatant Command, coalition, and inter-agency exercises. We also run a Cyber Wargame that looks five years into the future and includes industry and academic experts. USCYBERCOM's flagship exercises, CYBER FLAG and CYBER GUARD, are much more sophisticated now and are coupled directly with Joint Doctrine and the Force Model. CYBER FLAG, held each fall at Nellis Air Force Base in

Nevada, includes all the Service cyber components as well as inter-agency and international partners. CYBER FLAG 14 in November 2013 assembled more than 800 participants, included conventional maneuvers and kinetic fires in conjunction with cyber operations, and featured a much more realistic and aggressive adversary in its expanded virtual battlespace. In the past we were tentative about letting the cyber "red teams" loose, for fear they would impair expensive training opportunities for conventional arms. In our recent CYBER FLAG iteration last fall, we figuratively took the gloves off. Our defense consequently got its collective nose bloodied, but the defenders to their credit fought back and prevailed in chasing a determined foe out of our systems. For its part, CYBER GUARD is a whole-of-government event exercising state- and national-level responses to adversary actions against critical infrastructure in a virtual environment. It brings together DHS, FBI, USCYBERCOM, state government officials, Information Sharing and Analysis Centers, and private industry participants at the tactical level to promote shared awareness and coordination to mitigate and recover from an attack while assessing potential federal cyber responses. Finally, we are also building and deploying tools of direct use to "conventional" commanders in kinetic operations, some of which were most recently utilized in the latest Red Flag exercise run to keep our pilots at the highest degree of proficiency.

Where Are We Going?

Let me share with you my vision for what we at USCYBERCOM are building toward. We all know the US military is a force in transition. We are shifting away from legacy weapons, concepts, and missions, and seeking to focus—in a constrained resource environment—on being ready for challenges from old and new technologies, tensions, and adversaries. We have to fulfill traditional-style missions at the same time that we prepare for emerging ones, with new tools, doctrines, and expectations, both at home and abroad. We are grateful to Congress for lessening the threat of wholesale budget cuts called for by the Budget control Act. That makes it easier for the Department of Defense to maintain its determination to shield our cyberspace capabilities from the resource reductions falling on other areas of the total force. It is fair, and indeed essential, for you to ask how we are utilizing such resources while others are cutting back.

Our answer is that the trained and certified teams of our Cyber Mission Force are already improving our defenses and expanding the operational options for national decision makers, the Department's leadership, and joint force commanders. We are building this force and aligning the missions of the teams with intelligence capabilities and military requirements. Our cyber mission teams will bring even more capability to the "joint fight" and to whole-of-government and international efforts:

- USCYBERCOM is working with the Joint Staff and the combatant commands to capture their cyber requirements and to implement and refine interim guidance on the command and control of cyber forces "in-theater," ensuring our cyber forces provide direct and effective support to commanders' missions while also helping USCYBERCOM in its national-level missions. In addition, we are integrating our efforts and plans with component command operational plans, and we want to ensure that this collaboration continues at all the Commands.

- Our new operating concept to enhance military cyber capabilities is helping to foster a whole-of-government approach to counter our nation's cyber adversaries. Indeed, USCYBERCOM planners, operators, and experts are prized for their ability to bring partners together to conceptualize and execute operations like those that had significant effects over the last year in deterring and denying our adversaries' cyber designs.

Here is my greatest concern as I work to prepare my successor and move toward retirement. Despite our progress at USCYBERCOM, I worry that we might not be ready in time. Threats to our nation in cyberspace are growing. We are working to ensure that we would see any preparations for a devastating cyber attack on our critical infrastructure or economic system, but we also know that warning is never assured and often not timely enough for effective preventive actions. Should an attack get through, or if a provocation were to escalate by accident into a major cyber incident, we at USCYBERCOM expect to be called upon to defend the nation. We plan and train for this every day. My Joint Operations Center team routinely conducts and practices its Emergency Action Procedures to defend the nation through inter-agency emergency cyber procedures. During these conferences, which we have exercised with the participation up to the level of the Deputy Secretary of Defense, we work with our interagency partners to determine if a Cyber Event, Threat or Attack has occurred or will occur through cyberspace against the United States. As Commander, USCYBERCOM, I make an assessment of the likelihood of an attack and recommendations to take, if applicable. We utilize this process in conjunction with the National Military Command Center (NMCC) to determine when and if the conference should transition to a National Event or Threat Conference.

We understand that security is one of the greatest protections for civil liberties, and that liberty can suffer when governments hastily adapt measures after attacks. At USCYBERCOM we do our work in full support and defense of the civil liberties and privacy of Americans. We do not see a tradeoff between security and liberty; we promote both simultaneously, because each enhances

48

the other. Personnel at USCYBERCOM take this responsibility very seriously.
The tools, authorities, and culture of compliance at NSA/CSS give us the
ability and the confidence to achieve operational success against some of the
toughest national security targets while acting in a manner consistent with civil
liberties and rights to privacy. That said, unless Congress moves to enact
cybersecurity legislation to enable the private sector to share with the US
Government the anomalous cyber threat activity detected on its networks on a
real-time basis, we will remain handicapped in our ability to assist the private
sector or defend the nation in the event of a real cyber attack. I urge you to
consider the now daily reports of hostile cyber activity against our nation's
networks and appreciate the very real threat they pose to our nation's
economic and national security as well as our citizen's personal information. I
am concerned that this appreciation has been lost over the last several months,
as has the understanding that—when performed with appropriate safeguards—
cyber threat information sharing actually enhances the privacy and civil
liberties as well as the security of our citizens.

Conclusion

Thank you again, Mr. Chairman and Members of the Committee, for
inviting me to speak, and for all the help that you and this Committee have
provided USCYBERCOM over the years. It has been my honor to work in
partnership with you for these past 39+ years to build our nation's defenses.
Never before has our nation assembled the talent, resources, and authorities
that we have now started building into a cyber force. I am excited about the
work we have done and the possibilities before us. This is changing our
nation's capabilities, and making us stronger and better able to defend
ourselves across the board, and not merely in cyberspace. We can all be proud
of what our efforts have accomplished in building USCYBERCOM and
positioning its men and women, and my successor, for continued progress and
success.

Biography - Commander, U.S. Cyber Command, Director, National Security Agency/Chief, Central Security Service

GEN Keith B. Alexander
United States Army

General Keith B. Alexander, USA, is the Commander, U.S. Cyber Command (USCYBERCOM) and Director, National Security Agency/Chief, Central Security Service (NSA/CSS), Fort George G. Meade, MD. As Commander, USCYBERCOM, he is responsible for planning, coordinating and conducting operations and defense of DoD computer networks as directed by USSTRATCOM. As the Director of NSA and Chief of CSS, he is responsible for a Department of Defense agency with national foreign intelligence, combat support, and U.S. national security information system protection responsibilities. NSA/CSS civilian and military personnel are stationed worldwide.

He was born in Syracuse, NY, and entered active duty at the U.S. Military Academy at West Point.

Previous assignments include the Deputy Chief of Staff (DCS, G-2), Headquarters, Department of the Army, Washington, DC; Commanding General of the U.S. Army Intelligence and Security Command at Fort Belvoir, VA; Director of Intelligence, United States Central Command, MacDill Air Force Base, FL.; and Deputy Director for Requirements, Capabilities, Assessments and Doctrine, J-2, for the Joint Chiefs of Staff. GEN Alexander has served in a variety of command assignments in Germany and the United States. These include tours as Commander of Border Field Office, 511th MI Battalion, 66th MI Group; 336th Army Security Agency Company, 525th MI Group; 204th MI Battalion; and 525th MI Brigade.

Additionally, GEN Alexander held key staff assignments as Deputy Director and Operations Officer, Army Intelligence Master Plan, for the Deputy Chief of Staff for Intelligence; S-3 and Executive Officer, 522nd MI Battalion, 2nd Armored Division; G-2 for the 1st Armored Division both in Germany and Operation DESERT SHIELD/DESERT STORM in Saudi Arabia.

GEN Alexander holds a Bachelor of Science degree from the U.S. Military Academy and a Master of Science degree in Business Administration from Boston University. He holds a Master of Science degree in Systems Technology (Electronic Warfare) and a Master of Science degree in Physics from the naval Post Graduate School. He also holds a Master of Science degree in National Security Strategy from the National Defense University. His military education includes the Armor Officer Basic Course, the Military Intelligence Officer Advanced Course, the U.S. Army Command and General Staff College, and the National War College.

His badges include the Senior Parachutist Badge, the Army Staff Identification Badge, and the Joint Chief of Staff Identification Badge.

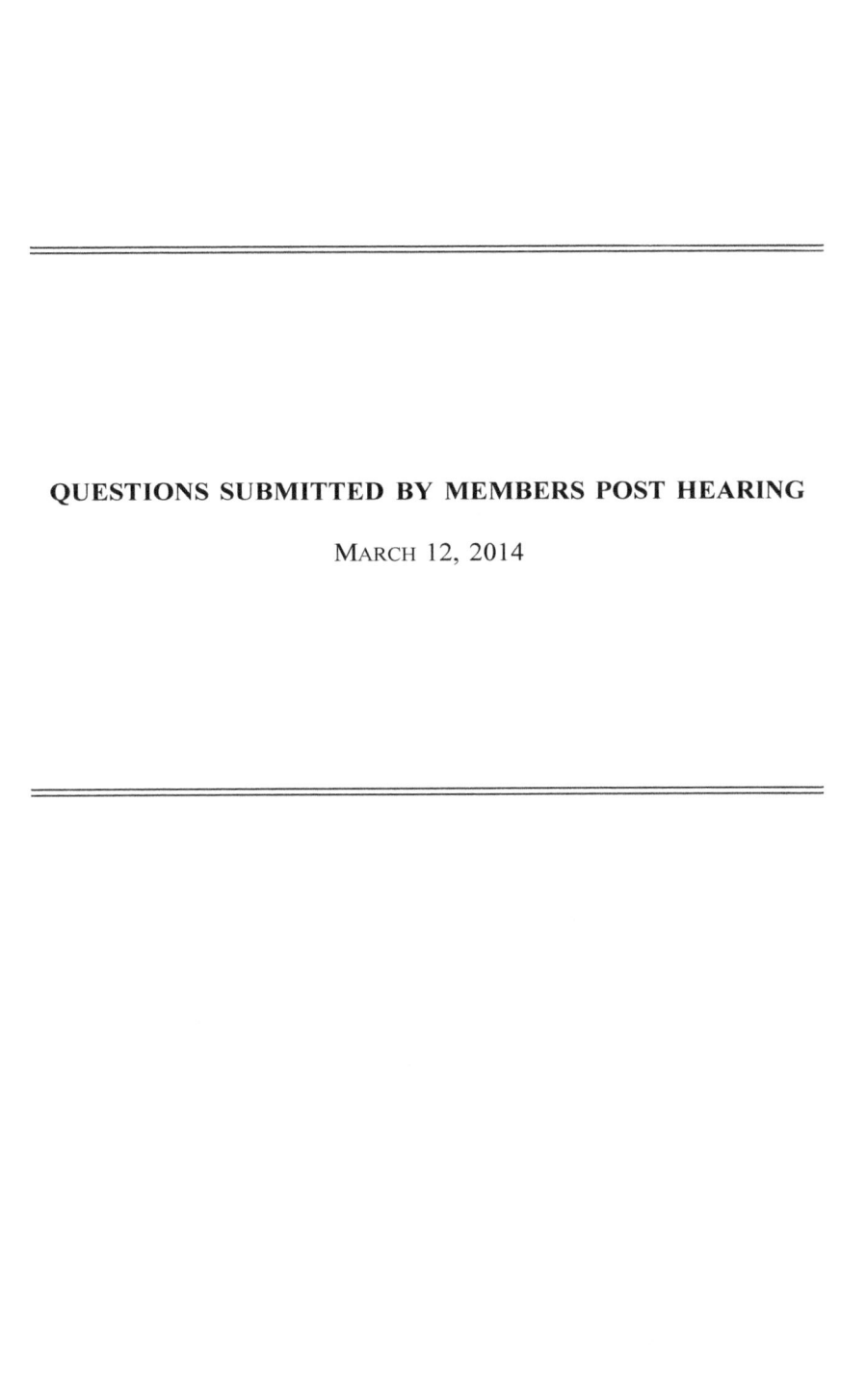

QUESTIONS SUBMITTED BY MEMBERS POST HEARING

MARCH 12, 2014

QUESTIONS SUBMITTED BY MR. THORNBERRY

Mr. THORNBERRY. Can you describe how the recommendations from the review by former Secretary of the Air Force Donley affect the governance and acquisition of IT and cyber systems for DOD? What actions have been taken to date to implement those recommendations?

Ms. TAKAI. I am working closely with the Deputy Chief Management Officer and the Under Secretary of Defense for Acquisition, Technology and Logistics on the recommendations of former Secretary Donley. As part of this effort, we are reviewing existing IT governance processes to ensure they enable more rapid delivery and sustainment of information technology and cyber capabilities. We will ensure that Congress is kept apprised of our efforts throughout this process.

Mr. THORNBERRY. How are we instrumenting and architecting our infrastructure so as to better detect, mitigate, and recover from deep insider threats? How are you ensuring that such investments are efficient (effective and economical)?

Ms. TAKAI. The cybersecurity of our networks is one of our top missions and we are giving it the serious attention it deserves. Our Insider Threat efforts are in alignment with guidance from the White House's Senior Information Sharing and Safeguarding Steering Committee and the President's National Insider Threat Policy and Minimum Standards. The Department has made good progress in implementing the Steering Committee's priority efforts.

There are two examples of specific architectural efforts we have implemented to better detect, mitigate and recover from insider threats. First, we have completed deployment of the Host Based Security System (HBSS) which enables monitoring of networks for suspicious user behavior. Second, we are also near 90% complete in implementing use of Public Key Infrastructure (PKI) hard-token certificates for our Secret network user authentication. PKI use is the cornerstone to eliminating anonymity, so that user actions can be monitored and irrefutably attributed to the individual users, thus helping to detect and deter malicious insiders.

Based on the most recent unauthorized disclosures of classified information, in July 2013, the Undersecretary of Defense for Intelligence and I issued a memorandum directing stronger mitigations for insider threat, including: two-person controls over use of removable media and the requirement to revalidate the need for privileged users, such as system administrators, in order to reduce the potential risk these users may pose. We are about to issue additional guidance which includes oversight of privileged users and stronger access controls over our most sensitive information to restrict access to those with a "need to know".

In order to ensure that our IT investments to counter insider threats are efficient (effective and economical), all our investments are vetted and validated through our existing governance processes. This is especially true now due to our constrained budget environment.

Mr. THORNBERRY. What activities does DOD have underway, or is contemplating beginning this year, related to making its systems more spectrum efficient?

Ms. TAKAI. Successful implementation of the DOD Alternative Proposal for the 1755–1780 MHz band is based on making systems more spectrum efficient. As such, a number of the proposals in the 1755–1780 MHz band Transition Plans are planned to do exactly that.

In addition, DOD recently released an Electromagnetic Spectrum Strategy that identifies goals to improve spectrum access opportunities, including developing systems that are efficient, flexible, and adaptable in their spectrum use and increasing our operational agility in use of the spectrum. To implement the Strategy, DOD is developing a roadmap and action plan over the next six months that will lay out near- to long-term milestones, including those related to sharing opportunities.

Mr. THORNBERRY. What opportunities do you see for the commercial sector to be more spectrally efficient with the spectrum bands it already has?

Ms. TAKAI. The Department of Defense is working closely with the National Telecommunications and Information Administration, Federal Communications Commission, Office of Science and Technology Policy and wireless industry stakeholders to evaluate and identify ways to share spectrum with commercial users, when possible. At the same time, the commercial sector could equally be more efficient in its use of non-Federal bands by providing opportunities for Department of Defense and other Federal government users to share spectrum, when possible, to meet growing mission requirements.

Specifically as a first step to facilitate the opportunity for bi-direction sharing, the Department of Defense, National Telecommunications and Information Administration, and the National Science Foundation are working together to pursue an Other Transaction Agreement with an eligible entity to develop and mature technologies and related policy changes to enable advanced approaches to spectrum use. The intent is to explore the creation of a forum that facilitates collaboration across government, industry and academia on spectrum technology development, including for shared uses between Federal and private sector operations. Industry support of this and similar efforts is critical in order to support the nation's growing economic and national security demands on spectrum.

Mr. THORNBERRY. How are we instrumenting and architecting our infrastructure so as to better detect, mitigate, and recover from deep insider threats? How are you ensuring that such investments are efficient (effective and economical)?

General ALEXANDER. In July 2013 the Commander, USCYBERCOM, organized a working group dedicated to insider threat mitigation. The working group comprised representatives from USCYBERCOM, NSA, DISA, DOD CIO, DIA, DSS, and the Service Cyber components. The team synchronized its efforts with the release of the USD(I) and DOD CIO memorandum "Insider Threat Mitigation" on 12 July 2013, which provided the opportunity to further operationalize current policies and expand guidance in accordance with USCYBERCOM's authorities. Understanding that there is no "silver bullet" to mitigate the insider threat, the mitigation strategy depended on a combination of technical solutions, policy, legal and cultural adjustments. A constant throughout all efforts is eventual alignment with the security architecture under the Joint Information Environment (JIE). The initial quick look study, which was presented to the DepSecDef, leveraged several previous assessments, studies and policies to identify "best of breed" tactics, techniques and procedures for immediate implementation with follow on development to institutionalize mid-term and long-term tasks. The study resulted in an order from USCYBERCOM to the DOD enterprise to mitigate common vulnerabilities associated with insider threat. Compliance with this order was achieved by 30 October 2013. CYBERCOM briefed the OpsDepsTank and the Chairman's Tank in December 2013. As a result, a SecDef memo, Task Force to Review Compromise of Classified Information, was signed out on 7 March 2014. Based on that memo four distinct lines of effort are under development:

a. Two-person integrity controls for the SIPRNET

b. A tiered non-compliance consequence matrix, which is being written and tested by the Marine Corps

c. Patch and Security Technical Implementation Guidance (STIG) for Programs of Record

d. An order to the DOD enterprise directing a number of technical changes, which will include tasks directed by the 11 Feb 14 White House memo, Near Term Measures to Reduce the Risk of High Impact Unauthorized Disclosures, and mid-term mitigations that will take a longer period of time to implement.

Among the tasks to be directed, the following concepts will be operationalized:

a. Increased scrutiny on the separation of duties among privileged users

b. Isolation of logged privileged user activities, storing logs out of reach of privileged users

c. Privileged user log review conducted by an Insider Threat team or other external entity

d. Reduced reliance on removable media by requiring use of cross domain solutions when practicable

e. Continued fine tuning of the Host Based Security System to identify unauthorized attempts to use removable media

Other pending efforts include a planned brief to CAPE, incorporating the new efforts into inspection programs and continued support to the Mitigation Oversight Task Force (MOTF), which is run by the Joint Staff.

Since these new requirements are unfunded, the timeliness of compliance may be an issue and implementation will most likely occur during regularly scheduled upgrades or as part of an overarching program implementation such as JIE.

Mr. THORNBERRY. To what extent has U.S. Cyber Command collected measures of performance or measures of effectiveness to demonstrate that the dual-hatted position is the most effective and most efficient approach to both agencies missions?

General ALEXANDER. While measures of performance and measures of effectiveness have utility in specific operations and processes we carry out at the tactical level, none have yet been defined for the Commander, USCYBERCOM and Director,

National Security Agency dual hat relationship. The dual hat relationship is prompted not just by a drive for efficiencies but also by operational necessity and the need for unity of effort in cyberspace. The lack of historical data on alternative relationships for command in cyberspace and the difficulty of empirically measuring concepts like "unity of command" would make deriving and evaluating measures of performance or effectiveness for the dual hat problematic.

Mr. THORNBERRY. Could you please describe the command and control relationships between U.S. Cyber Command and the other combatant commands and the degree to which the new rules of engagement have had any impact on this.

General ALEXANDER. [The information is for official use only and retained in the committee files.]

———

QUESTIONS SUBMITTED BY MR. CARSON

Mr. CARSON. How has the NSA/DHS Centers of Academic Excellence in Information Assurance program impacted your access to qualified candidates for cybersecurity positions? What lessons have been learned from this program? And are there opportunities to share these lessons, either in curriculum recommendations or some other format, with universities and colleges that are not Centers of Excellence so they can provide consistent education?

Ms. TAKAI. The NSA/DHS Centers of Academic Excellence in Information Assurance program has facilitated development of the pipeline of educated candidates for cybersecurity positions. Since 2001 the National Centers of Academic Excellence (CAE) in Information Assurance have employed 593 Information Assurance Scholarship Program (IASP)/CAE graduates (a 97% completion rate from the 608 scholarships awarded) and sponsored 216 capacity building grants with CAEs. The IASP provides DOD both new hires upon graduation (recruiting) and opportunities for current DOD IA Workforce members to advance their education (retention).

With the publication of the National Initiative for Cybersecurity Education (NICE) workforce framework and the evolutionary nature of the cyberspace workforce, now is the time to evaluate the CAE program. My office is currently leading a study and analysis of the CAE process, on behalf of DOD, in response to the FY14 National Defense Authorization Act direction. As part of this analysis, an assessment of lessons learned is being conducted. A report with the overall assessment of the CAE program and our recommendations will be generated and shared.

Additionally, there are public venues (e.g., Colloquium for Information Systems Security Education (CISSE) and the National Initiative for Cybersecurity Education (NICE) conference) which allow participants to partner and mentor fellow CAE institutions and those aspiring to become CAEs. Workshops are held on mapping courses, partnership and scholarship opportunities, ultimately discussing what's working and not working; and collecting feedback on improvement of CAE processes.

Mr. CARSON. How has the NSA/DHS Centers of Academic Excellence in Information Assurance program impacted your access to qualified candidates for cybersecurity positions? What lessons have been learned from this program? And are there opportunities to share these lessons, either in curriculum recommendations or some other format, with universities and colleges that are not Centers of Excellence so they can provide consistent education?

General ALEXANDER. The National Centers of Academic Excellence in Information Assurance (CAE) have provided outstanding and highly sought candidates for DOD Information Assurance/Cybersecurity positions. NSA Recruiters actively recruit from the 181 National Centers of Academic Excellence (CAE) to hire qualified candidates into our IA/Cyber positions. In addition, our Components actively seek students from CAEs applying for the DOD Information Assurance Scholarship Program (IASP). The IASP provides both new DOD hires upon graduation (recruiting) and opportunities for current DOD IA Workforce members to advance their education (retention). Some specific advantages of the IASP are:

- Scholarships are tied to a DOD position and are awarded to students attending CAEs
- Continuous flow of top IA talent meeting DOD requirements
- Students participate in internship programs during academic breaks within the community to learn DOD systems and procedures
- Graduates have a commitment to serve in the DOD for a specified time after graduation (dependent on length of scholarship)

Since 2001, DOD has employed 503 IASP/CAE graduates with a 97% completion rate (a total of 608 scholarships have been awarded) and sponsored 216 capacity building grants with CAEs. DOD works with CAEs to award grants to conduct curriculum development and research of interest to both the schools and DOD. CAE students and faculty participate in these grant projects. Through these grants, CAEs are encouraged to share their results with other CAEs, minority institutions, and institutions that may be seeking CAE designation. Many CAEs have held train-the-trainer and faculty development sessions at various conferences and events. NSA and DHS will conduct further research to determine the direct relationship between CAE alumni hiring and employment partnerships. Studies will also be conducted to determine whether CAE alumni are hired by government at a greater rate than non-CAE-graduates. NSA and DHS work with government, industry and academia throughout the year to identify skill gaps between education and job qualification/skills to ensure that CAE graduates are prepared to perform technical mission-critical Cybersecurity jobs. These gaps are then communicated to the CAEs with recommendations. NSA and DHS also utilize lessons learned to update the CAE program as required to meet the changing IA/Cybersecurity standards and the national demands in cyber defense. As a result of the most recent study, the CAE program was updated in 2013 and now includes Cyber Defense (CD) education. Academic institutions are now required to meet Core Knowledge Units (KU) and can apply for optional Focus Areas (FAs). Government, industry and the CAEs were involved in the update of the CAE program and will continue to evolve the program as national IA/Cybersecurity needs change. In the future, a NSA/DHS Advisory Council consisting of CAEs, industry and government partners will discuss potential changes to the CASE requirements. Updates to the requirements will allow the schools to keep up-to-date on curriculum and teaching methods within the Cybersecurity field. Under the 2014 National Defense Authorization Act (NDAA), DOD/CIO in partnership with NSA and DHS, is conducting an assessment of the NSA/DHS CAE program. The assessment will identify the CAE Program's strengths and weaknesses; processes and criteria; maturity of IA as an academic discipline; the government's role in the future development of the CAE curricula and criteria; advantages and disadvantages of broadening the governance structure of CAEs; and the alignment of CAE curricula/criteria to the National Initiative for Cybersecurity Education (NICE). NSA and DHS along with other government agencies, industry and academia speak at several venues during the year to brief the CAE program, lessons learned and to convey the national IA/Cybersecurity requirements. Annually, NSA and DHS attend the Colloquium for Information Systems Security Education (CISSE), the NICE conference and the CAE Principal's meeting. These venues allow participants to partner and mentor fellow CAE institutions and those aspiring to become CAEs. Workshops are held for aspirants on mapping courses to the CAE Criteria, along with partnership and scholarship opportunities. The National Science Foundation (NSF) Advanced Technological Education (ATE) centers reach out to potential 2-year institutions through curriculum sharing and mentoring by 4-year schools. For example, one of the STE centers—CyberWatch—has hosted several webinars to educate interested CAEs and non-CAEs on the new Information Assurance/Cyber Defense criteria. Webinars were selected for the collaboration amongst attendees.

————

QUESTIONS SUBMITTED BY MR. KILMER

Mr. KILMER. The Department is looking to consolidate into a one size fits all desktop solution in the cloud run through DISA, known as virtual desktop infrastructure. Currently, each Service is running on various desktop solutions. Can you explain how the Department is incorporating the unique needs of the user from each Service into this infrastructure?

Ms. TAKAI. The Defense Information Systems Agency (DISA) recently concluded a virtual desktop infrastructure (VDI) proof-of-concept that examined the value of VDI for DISA's desktop computing requirements. DISA is currently analyzing the outcomes of this initial proof-of-concept to inform decisions on the future approach to desktop computing within the DISA organization, but no decision has been made to consolidate into a one size fits all desktop solution in the cloud. Similar efforts are underway across the DOD Components, but each is looking at the specific desktop computing needs within that Component.

While the Department will look into the feasibility and effectiveness of providing a VDI solution, currently, there are no enterprise efforts underway. Such an effort, if undertaken, would need to address the challenge of supporting any unique user or organization needs.

Mr. KILMER. Defense Information Systems Agency (DISA) appears to be leading IT centralization efforts in the Department. A cornerstone of this effort is the highly publicized but not widely understood Joint Information Environment (JIE). Can you discuss JIE's and DISA's role in the future of IT in DOD?

Ms. TAKAI. My office is overseeing the implementation of JIE, which is being implemented by and through the DOD Components, including DISA as a key player. The primary goals of the JIE are to make the Department more effective and more secure against cyber threats, to reduce cost associated with the Department's overall information technology infrastructure by simplifying, standardizing, centralizing, and automating infrastructure at the enterprise level.

The JIE will improve mission effectiveness by ensuring timely and secure access to data and services regardless of location or device; maintaining access to information/services in the face of network disruption, degradation, or damage; and enabling rapid and dynamic capability evolution to meet mission needs across all operational scenarios. JIE will enhance the Department's cybersecurity by providing a consistent IT architecture that improves network resiliency and defensibility, and network operators and defenders with shared situation awareness. Finally, JIE enables more efficient use of resources by reducing duplication of effort across Components, reducing total IT operating costs, and supporting more rapid fielding of new IT capabilities within a standardized IT architecture.

DISA is a key player in the development, implementation and operation of the IT infrastructure that enables JIE for the Department. They specifically support the JIE effort by developing technical architectures; developing, implementing and operating many of the JIE related capabilities such as networking, security, computing services, enterprise services, and network operations centers; and providing engineering expertise needed to enable the Department to leverage commercial technologies and to integrate new technologies into the JIE architecture.

Mr. KILMER. The Department of Defense has entered into numerous cross-Service contracts and has increased the utilization of enterprise license agreements. Can you outline the future of these contracts, how the offices responsible for negotiating these contracts are designated, and how these offices gather regular input from the Services for their unique requirements?

Ms. TAKAI. The Department of Defense is conducting a DOD-wide inventory of selected software licenses inventory in accordance with fiscal year 2013 National Defense Authorization Act direction. The selected software list was established from an analysis of acquisition data that identified publishers with high IT spend across DOD. The selected inventory will help identify future targets for enterprise license agreements.

The DOD Enterprise Software Initiative (ESI) Working Group is the primary method of setting the strategic sourcing opportunities for the Department. DOD ESI coordinates and manages enterprise software agreements to leverage DOD spend for volume discounts and optimize license use and contract terms and conditions. My office, with support from the Defense Information Systems Agency (DISA) and DOD Components, is pursuing Department-wide Enterprise License Agreements (ELA's) that will improve operational efficiencies and enhance cybersecurity and interoperability across DOD while lowering the total cost of ownership for software. Currently we are pursuing ELA's with CISCO and VMware while working the business case analysis with Components.

Given their expertise and role in contracting and procurement of information technology, DISA is leading the Department's efforts for coordinating and negotiating DOD-wide ELAs, with the Components providing their specific requirements and funding. DISA works with the Components to establish licensing models and associated transition plans to achieve effective DOD-wide ELAs for software that is selected based on sound business case analyses (BCAs) which document the cost savings, cost efficiencies and other benefits and risks of establishing DOD-wide ELAs.

In addition, several Components have created large Joint Enterprise License Agreements (JELAs) that we plan to leverage and incorporate into DOD-wide ELAs in the future.

Mr. KILMER. The Department of Defense is looking to adopt more cloud computing capabilities but also has a unique set of security requirements that not all vendors will be able to comply. How do you drive competition into the cloud market and ensure a level playing field for competitors so the Department can ensure best value for the service?

Ms. TAKAI. The Department gains significant benefit from commercial innovations and ongoing competition. To ensure a level playing field and increased completion, the Department is making significant investments to promote the use of commercial cloud services, categorize our cybersecurity requirements, and speed-up our assessment and approval processes.

My office designated the Defense Information Systems Agency (DISA) as the Enterprise Cloud Service Broker (ECSB) to promote the access and use of cloud service providers (CSPs), to consolidate enterprise demand to maximize the Department's buying power, and facilitate and optimize the DOD's access and use of commercial cloud services that can meet our security and interoperability requirements.

The DOD has developed a Cloud Security Model that defines six security impact levels (public release through and including Secret) and the requirements the CSP needs to meet (at each level) in order to integrate with the Department's cybersecurity processes and architecture without requiring each prospective CSP to operate at the highest level. The Federal Risk and Authorization Management Program (FedRAMP) is a government-wide program providing a standardized approach to security assessment, authorization, and continuous monitoring for cloud services and uses a ''do once, use many times'' assessment process to reduce cost, time, and staff for both the CSP and the government. OMB policy requires Federal departments and agencies to comply with FedRAMP guidelines by June 2014.

The ECSB leverages FedRAMP packages and considers commercial equivalencies to DOD-specific security requirements throughout its assessment process. In this way, a CSP can work towards FedRAMP compliance and target a specific DOD Cloud Security Model security impact level for their service knowing that other CSPs need to meet the same set of requirements. The CSP is then free to compete, on a level playing field, for DOD business in a manner that meets the Department's security requirements and provides best overall value.

Mr. KILMER. The FBI issued a consumer alter this summer regarding the growing threat of malware in pirated software. What is the Department of Defense doing to with its contractors and subcontractors to ensure its supply chain does not procure pirated software, thereby opening up a potential side door cyber security threat for the Department of Defense?

Ms. TAKAI. DOD is actively working to improve its software assurance practices internally through a Software Assurance Community of Practice (SwA COP), as well as working on standards and best practices in concert with public-private groups (e.g., The Open Group, Consortium of IT Software Quality. DOD is incorporating best practices, such as buying from authorized channels whenever possible and identifying purchase options for sustainment procurements to ensure product authenticity and identification of trusted sources. There are also on-going efforts within DOD and across the inter-agency and commercial communities to develop standardized contract language for product integrity expectations and associated liabilities, as well as mutually recognized product or organizational certifications. DOD and the National Security Agency are monitoring development of the Software Identification Tag Standard (ISO/IEC 19770). Though not fully adopted by the private sector or government, there is growing interest and support to adopt this standard, and it could be very useful in securing the software supply chain.

Additionally, DOD is working with General Services Administration (GSA) and other interagency partners on ways to implement recommendations in the DOD and GSA Report, ''Improving Cybersecurity and Resilience through the Acquisition Process,'' (January 23, 2014).

Mr. KILMER. In the past year, the Department of Defense has initiated several rulemakings focused on stronger procurement policies and supply chain controls [DFARS 2012–D055, DFARS 2012–D050, etc]. Given the growing body of data demonstrating that counterfeit software often comes bundled with malware that can cause cybersecurity risks, this is a growing area of concern for the Department. What is the path forward on these policies and how else is the Department considering explicitly addressing the risks associated with contractors' use of counterfeit software?

Ms. TAKAI. As part of DOD's larger Cybersecurity and Trusted Systems and Networks strategies, the Department recognizes the importance of purchasing information technology with adequate cybersecurity built in. As such, DOD is updating its procurement policy to reflect the global, commercial marketplace from which DOD procures technology to implement critical missions. These procurement policies represent one set of mitigation tools in the cybersecurity toolbox.

  • DFARS Case 2012–D055, Requirements Relating to Supply Chain Risk, implements Section 806 of the National Defense Authorization Act of 2011. Defense Procurement and Acquisition Policy and the DOD CIO are in the process of modifying the interim rule based on comments received from industry and Congress. In addition, DOD is identifying pilot programs to exercise the new policy, once revised.

  • DFARS Case 2012–D055, Detection and Avoidance of Counterfeit Electronic Parts. The draft final rule is at the Office of Management and Budget's Office of Information and Regulatory Affairs for clearance to be published in the Federal Register.

- DFARS Case 2014–D005, Detection and Avoidance of Counterfeit Electronic Parts—Further Implementation. The draft proposed rule is in the initial drafting phase.
- DOD continues to work with GSA and other interagency partners to develop an implementation plan supporting the final report of the Department of Defense (DOD) and General Services Administration (GSA) Joint Working Group on Improving Cybersecurity and Resilience through Acquisition, signed by the Secretary of Defense and the Administrator of General Services on January 23, 2014.

My office is also leading or co-leading several internal efforts to share information and develop best practices in this area. A few examples are:
- The DOD Software Assurance (SwA) Community of Practice, a group of DOD SwA practitioners, share information on software assurance best practices to be leveraged in improving guidance to the Department's Program Protection processes.
- DOD is also involved in industry-government information sharing effort to flag potential counterfeit issues through the Government-Industry Data Exchange Program (GIDEP).
- DOD is exploring "track and trace" technologies that may afford manufacturers, distributors, and acquirers the capability to better validate authenticity of parts and components.

Mr. KILMER. The current DOD Certification and Accreditation (C&A) of software is a fragmented process between DOD Service components and is often not standardized for all vendors. This often results in delayed and inconsistent certification and accreditation of IT products, as well as delays the customers' deployment and subsequent time to value for software acquisition. In the past, this process has taken over a year which has fostered inefficient deployment of systems procured and incentivizes DOD organizations to procure redundant systems. What is the Department doing to streamline and standardize the C&A process?

Ms. TAKAI. My office recently published DODI 8500.01 "Cybersecurity," and DODI 8510.01 "Risk Management Framework for DOD IT" which transitions the Department from the DOD-specific Defense Information Assurance Certification and Accreditation Process (DIACAP) to the National Institute of Standards and Technology (NIST) Risk Management Framework (RMF) and the NIST security controls, which are already in use by the rest of the Federal Government. Vendors may now build products once according to NIST guidelines and then more readily deploy them government-wide.

DOD's alignment with the Civil and Intelligence Community on NIST guidelines creates one standard that will streamline interagency information system interconnectivity and promote information sharing. The policies also stress incorporation of cybersecurity early and robustly in the acquisition and system development lifecycle, reducing time and money spent bolting security on late in system development, and producing material with cyber security that can keep up with an evolving threat. The policies also establish NIST's concept of "common controls," allowing information systems to inherit existing controls from hosting organizations, reducing the number of controls that must be implemented by individual information systems. Additionally, individual software "products" are not subject to the full RMF process an information system undergoes. Products are securely configured in accordance with security controls applicable to that particular product, and then undergo assessment prior to incorporation into an information system. With the adoption of the common NIST guidelines, product vendors will be able to better understand cybersecurity requirements before they begin development, ensuring streamlined approval by DOD.

Mr. KILMER. The DNI and CIA recognized that they could not afford to build a community, multi-tenant cloud with the innovations, scale and capabilities that already exist via the leading commercial cloud providers, and that is was faster, cheaper, and better to leverage industry. My understanding is DISA is attempting to build their own cloud solution called milCloud which would likely be directly competitive to Commercial Cloud Providers (CSPs)? How much are you spending to build this solution, and more importantly, why are you not following the same logic the intelligence community is using, even for classified data?

Ms. TAKAI. Under the Intelligence Community Information Technology Enterprise (IC ITE) effort, DNI is pursuing both commercially provided and Government provided private cloud capabilities. While the large public cloud vendors have certainly captured everyone's attention, other commercial companies have made significant investments to provide products that enable organizations to implement their own private cloud environments. These products have matured to a point where establishing a private cloud environment is no longer the difficult undertaking that it once was. In fact, many of these products build on an organizations existing infrastructure to provide cloud capabilities.

The genesis of milCloud stemmed from actions to drive efficiencies and automation into an enterprise computing service. Today, milCloud's IaaS capability is implemented using commercial products that build on DISA's existing, commercially-provided and competitively acquired computing infrastructure, and enabled DISA to achieve an initial capability with minimal risk. The lessons learned in providing this initial capability are providing valuable information that is informing the Department's long term approach to achieving cloud capabilities.

The approach taken by the CIA is one of the models under consideration by the Department. One of the most interesting aspects of the CIA cloud is that they were able to attract a large public cloud vendor to provide a private cloud capability for the IC. Prior to this contract, Amazon had never provided this type of private cloud. The scope of the CIA contract created enough incentive to convince Amazon to entertain a new business model that they previously had not supported. Compared with the CIA's $80.6 million investment, DOD has invested approximately $4.7 million to establish the initial milCloud's IaaS capability.

Today, the Department is making small investments that are improving our understanding of which of the cloud acquisition models will deliver best value solutions to the Department's IT requirements. These investments are enabling us to develop a standard approach for integrating CSPs with our wide area network defenses and for conducting coordinated responses to cyber attacks. With these procedures and technologies, the Department will be able to scale to multiple commercial providers and gain efficiencies through competition and commercial innovation.

As we learn from our initial cloud efforts, define the appropriate cybersecurity constructs, and continue our collaboration with industry, the Department will be able to effectively expand our use of both public clouds and commercially-hosted private clouds.

Mr. KILMER. Why is DOD classifying all sensitive data/workloads that would run in a Commercial CSP as National Security Systems (NSS) and be subject to additional security controls, when very few of them are actually classified as NSS by definition?

Ms. TAKAI. The Department is not classifying all sensitive data and workloads as NSS. In our cybersecurity policies we do not differentiate between NSS and non-NSS. Rather, we have a single set of cybersecurity controls that is then tailored to a particular system based on the effect that system has on the Department's ability to perform its assigned mission, protect its assets, and fulfill its responsibilities.

The Department uses the standard cybersecurity controls defined in NIST Special Publication 800–53, Security and Privacy Controls for Federal Information Systems and Organizations. Building on the NIST standards, the Department worked with the Intelligence Community and DHS to develop additional guidance on control selection for evaluating IT systems within the NIST Risk Management Framework. This guidance was published through the Committee for National Security Systems, but it is used for all DOD systems not just NSS.

Mr. KILMER. The Office of the CIO recently issued Supplemental Guidance for the Department of Defense's Acquisition and Secure Use of Commercial Cloud Services. This Guidance adds additional security controls and processes that Commercial CSPs have to go through in order to provide cloud services to DOD components. Will DOD data centers run by DISA be put through the same level of third party scrutiny and accreditation as commercial CSPs are required to complete? If not, why?

Ms. TAKAI. DOD data centers are evaluated using the same cybersecurity controls, but are held to a higher standard than is being used by the DOD Enterprise Cloud Service Broker (ECSB). Currently, the ECSB is using the standard profiles for hosting systems that processes unclassified information and whose loss would not have a significant effect on the Department's mission. DOD data centers are evaluated against the requirements for hosting all DOD workloads, including classified systems, and systems whose loss would have a catastrophic impact on the Department's mission. In addition, the DOD data centers are required to follow additional cybersecurity guidance defined in the DISA Security Technical Implementation Guides (STIG).

The additional requirements that are identified in the DOD Cloud Security Model address the need and approach for integrating Commercial CSPs with the Department's cybersecurity defenses and cybersecurity operations. DOD data centers are fully integrated with these network protections and operations.

Mr. KILMER. The CIA is moving swiftly to field the Commercial Cloud Solution (C2S) to take advantage of the rapid agility and innovation of commercial cloud. My understanding is this community cloud will service the entire intelligence community and significantly reduce the costs of computing and infrastructure as well as enhance security and operational effectiveness. What are your plans to begin transitioning your investment from the NSA IC cloud to C2S to further reduce costs and take advantage of the investment the DNI/CIA is making in this community cloud based on commercial cloud services?

General ALEXANDER. Having an IC Cloud with two diverse, but complementary, implementations—one commercial and one government—is part of the IC ITE architecture established by the ODNI. NSA is working with CIA bi-weekly to ensure that NSA's IC–GOVCLOUD and CIA's C2S maximize all resources available for IC ITE users. With C2S becoming available in the later summer of 2014, we will have more opportunity to meet a customer's needs. NSA and CIA have developed the Joint Store Front which is the front door for an agency to request cloud services. The Joint Store Front will align the requests with resources to ensure that a customer's needs are validated and met. NSA and CIA have agreed to assess the right mix of cloud services provided by both GOVCLOUD and C2S after C2S has been operational for 6 months. This would give us better metrics to make an informed decision of the roadmaps ahead and capacity needed for both. The assessment is due to ODNI February 2015. For its part as a consumer of the IC Cloud, NSA will be a consumer of C2S capabilities where the economies so indicate. We expect that the primary focus of the IC–GOVCLOUD will remain data access, integration, and analytics, and our roadmap includes converging the functionality of the internal NSA Major System Acquisition clouds (MDR1 and MDR2) with the IC–GOVCLOUD to maximize the potential for integrating data across the IC.

———————

QUESTIONS SUBMITTED BY MR. PETERS

Mr. PETERS. The Federal Information Technology Acquisition Reform Act of 2014 (FITARA) (HR 1232) passed the House on February 25 and has been referred to both the Senate Armed Services Committee and the Senate Homeland Security and Governmental Affairs Committee. With or without FITARA, how will the DOD ensure that solicitations are based on open standards, technical requirements, and without brand name references? What is the DOD doing to ensure that fair and open practices are being followed to avoid the "lock-in" of a single vendor?

Ms. TAKAI. Independent of the Federal Information Technology Acquisition Reform Act, the Department has recently issued the Interim DOD Instruction 5000.02, acquisition policy, that establishes a policy framework by which DOD will acquire IT. The updated policy includes guidance on creating and sustaining a competitive environment that encourages improved performance and cost control for DOD systems. The policy also addresses the issue of the government maintaining rights to data associated with a delivered capability to ensure that proprietary data formats and exchanges do not lead to "lock-in".

In addition to the updated acquisition policy mentioned above, the Department has promoted the use of open systems and open systems architecture by issuing guidance, such as the "DOD Open Systems Architecture Contract Guidebook for Program Managers", and "Clarifying Guidance Regarding Open Source Software (OSS)". Furthermore, these guidelines for open systems architecture have been incorporated into the curriculum of the Defense Acquisition University.

With regard to open standards, the Department has had a long-standing requirement for programs to follow IT standards that are listed in the DOD IT Standards Registry (DISR). The standards listed in the DISR are managed through a rigorous governance process in which open commercial standards are considered for adoption first and foremost. My office will continue to work closely with the office of the Under Secretary of Defense for Acquisition, Technology and Logistics to ensure IT investments are based on performance and value while meeting the Department's mission and business requirements.

Mr. PETERS. Many industry stakeholders believe that DOD sole source justifications are provided without adequate market research or include arguments favoring the need to maintain a single vendor network. Are you aware of instances where sole source justification was provided without adequate market research or in favor of a single vendor? Please describe the steps DOD is taking to introduce alternative network vendors into DOD network infrastructure environment.

Ms. TAKAI. I am not aware of any instance where a sole source justification was provided without adequate market research.

DOD procurement officials are required to follow the procedures outlined in the Federal Acquisition Regulation (FAR) and the Defense FAR Supplement (DFARS), Part 10—Market Research, which requires market research for all procurement levels but the level of detail will vary based on the dollar amount and complexity of the procurement. In accordance with FAR Subpart 10.002, acquisitions begin with a description of the Government's needs stated in terms sufficient to allow conduct of market research. Market research is then conducted to determine if commercial items or nondevelopmental items are available to meet the Government's needs or could be modified to meet the Government's needs.

In accordance with FAR Subpart 6.302–1(c)—Only One Responsible Source and No Other Supplies or Services Will Satisfy Agency Requirements—Application for brand name descriptions, there may be cases where the use of a particular brand-name, product, or feature of a product, peculiar to one manufacturer is essential to the Government's requirements, thereby precluding consideration of a product manufactured by another company. In these cases, a justification and approval must be executed and posted with the solicitation.